Parenting

Your

Ad...

C...

Parenting
Your
Adopted
Child

A Positive Approach to Building a Strong Family

ANDREW ADESMAN, M.D.
with CHRISTINE ADAMEC

McGraw-Hill

New York   Chicago   San Francisco   Lisbon   London   Madrid   Mexico City
Milan   New Delhi   San Juan   Seoul   Singapore   Sydney   Toronto

The McGraw·Hill Companies

Library of Congress Cataloging-in-Publication Data

Adesman, Andrew.
 Parenting your adopted child : a positive approach to building a strong family / by Andrew Adesman with Christine Adamec.
  p.   cm.
 Includes bibliographical references and index.
 ISBN 0-07-140980-7
  1. Adoption—United States.   2. Parenting—United States.   I. Adamec, Christine A., 1949–   II. Title.

 HV875.55.A35   2004
 649′.1—dc22   2003025276

ISBN 0-07-140980-7

McGraw-Hill books are available at special quantity discounts to use as premiums and sales promotions, or for use in corporate training programs. For more information, please write to the Director of Special Sales, Professional Publishing, McGraw-Hill, Two Penn Plaza, New York, NY 10121-2298. Or contact your local bookstore.

$14.95

This book is printed on acid-free paper.

Andrew Adesman would like to dedicate this book to his wife Angela, for her enduring support, patience, and forbearance.

Christine Adamec would like to dedicate this book to her husband, John Adamec.

Contents

Part II As They Grow

Part III Talking About Adoption

Part IV Special Issues

Foreword

MANY FAMILIES FIND getting started with adoption difficult. Potential adopters have many unanswered questions, and the adoption process itself can be daunting. Once families set out seriously on the adoption path, however, they quickly discover useful information to help them, including books, websites, and adoption conferences. In the end, whether families wish to adopt from the United States or another country, the adoption process often turns out to be quite straightforward, although it may take some initial research. When they arrive home with their beloved new baby or older child, most parents breathe a sigh of relief, assuming that the hard part is done. Now all they have to do, they figure, is love their child and raise him or her as children have traditionally been raised. In the past, parents might have just ignored the fact of the child's adoption altogether.

Today's parents, many of whom adopt transracially or via open or semi-open adoptions, are too savvy to believe that they can ignore adoption. In fact, most realize almost immediately that while parenting a child who joined the family through adoption is in most ways no different than parenting one who joined the family through biology, a number of adoptive parenting questions emerge quickly. How much information about their child should they share with their immediate family? The school? The neighbors? When and how should they begin talking about adoption with their child? For all children, questions of family health history and genetic learning styles become important; and for those adopted via foster or international adoption, health and development issues can be significant almost immediately. For parents of transracially adopted children, how to create a positive ethnic identity, how to handle intrusive questions, and how to maintain ties to a country or culture of origin represent tremendous challenges as a child grows.

Despite the increasing acceptance of adoption (over 1.5 million children in the United States joined their families via adoption), adoption literature remains focused on the pre-adoption process. Good parenting information is still in short supply. For these reasons, *Parenting Your Adopted Child* fills a significant gap in the library of parenting information. Dr. Andrew Adesman and Christine Adamec tackle the tough issues head-on, neither pathologizing nor denying the difficult aspects of adoptive parenting, demonstrating the very balance that they recommend to their readers. *Parenting Your Adopted Child* is a welcome source of practical, useful parenting advice to parents and friends.

—Susan Caughman
Editor and publisher, *Adoptive Families* magazine

Acknowledgments

The authors would like to thank the following individuals for their assistance: Susan Caughman, publisher of *Adoptive Families* magazine in New York City; Susan Freivalds, founder and editorial advisor of *Adoptive Families* magazine; Esther Gwinnell, M.D., a psychiatrist in private practice in Portland, Oregon, and associate clinical professor of psychiatry at Oregon Health and Sciences University; Matt McGue, Ph.D., psychology professor and principal investigator of the Sibling Interaction and Behavior Study (SIBS) at the University of Minnesota in Minneapolis, Minnesota; Marie Mercer, reference librarian at the DeGroodt Public Library in Palm Bay, Florida; and Mary Beth Style, M.S.W., an adoption social worker from Centreville, Virginia.

The authors would like to offer special thanks to senior editor Judith McCarthy for her valuable comments, which considerably enhanced the book.

Dr. Adesman would also like to thank Dr. Philip Lanzkowsky and Mr. John Brandecker at Schneider Children's Hospital for their long-standing support, without which he would not have been able to take on a writing project such as this. In addition, he thanks Nancy Alfieri, whose everyday clinical and administrative assistance has been consistently invaluable. Lastly, he would like to acknowledge his three children—Marisa, Danielle, and Jason—who challenge and expand his own knowledge and wisdom about parenting each and every day.

Introduction

SOME PEOPLE HAVE asked my coauthor and me why an adoptive parent needs a book specifically on *adoptive* parenting, versus one on parenting in general. It's a good question. It's true that general parenting books can assist you with many parenting questions. In fact, some advice in this book would be useful for nonadoptive parents as well as adoptive parents. But adoptive parents do need their own book.

They need it because of the extra issues that overlay adoption, in large part because of societal misconceptions about adoption. Many people in our culture are affected by the media and sadly, adopted children are often depicted as pathetic beings and "troubled transplants." Adoptive parents also need an adoptive parenting book because friends and relatives often ask them intrusive questions, and they need advice on how to handle them.

But the best reason for an adoptive parenting book is to help you to help your child with issues that come up about adoption: for example, explaining adoption is difficult for many parents, and Chapter 11 tells how to explain adoption to your child at different ages. Your child will also need your advice on coping with relatives, peers, teachers, and others, and these issues are addressed in this book.

Taking the Common Sense Approach

This book is about common sense adoptive parenting, sorting out silly or potentially dangerous advice and learning to rely on your own eyes and ears, while also using the advice of sensible people such as your pediatrician.

You are likely to hear advice from two extreme polar opposite positions on adoption. At one end, some people think parenting an adopted child is exactly the same as parenting a child born to your family, and insist there's no difference at all between the two situations.

At the other extreme, you'll hear some advice from those who think parenting an adopted child is completely different from parenting a child born to you and that adoption issues are at the root of any problems that arise with the child. People who believe "adoption issues" loom large in every adopted child's life react very differently from those who think the adoptive status of the child is irrelevant.

I believe the best way to navigate the shoals and sandy beaches of adoptive parenthood is a balance between the adoption-is-all and the adoption-is-irrelevant views. Sometimes a child really is upset about an issue related to adoption, and sometimes it's something altogether different that's the problem. Realizing this is part of a common sense approach.

Basic Parenting Beliefs About Adoption Are Important

When you're parenting a child, your underlying views are very important and color everything you do with and about your child as she grows up. For example, if you think parenting an adopted child is completely different from raising a child born to you, when your child misbehaves, you may find yourself holding back on discipline. If she begs long and hard for what she wants, you may decide it's okay to give in to your child. After all, she was adopted, isn't that enough of a burden? Doesn't she deserve a break from life's hardships?

What if she was an abused child? Surely this child deserves to be given as much as possible, to counter the suffering she's endured. Doesn't she? The answer: it depends. All children need discipline as well as love. Sometimes their adoptive status needs to be considered and sometimes it doesn't. If your child suffered from abuse before the adoption, taking a rigidly punitive attitude toward her when she misbehaves may worsen her behavior. Yet you shouldn't let the child "run wild," trying to somehow atone for bad experiences caused by others who harmed your child before you knew her.

Conversely, let's say you think an adopted child is no different from any other child. This underlying premise also affects how you parent your child. If you think adoptedness is not important because you're certain you treat your child the same way you'd treat a child born to you, you may fail to recognize that sometimes an aspect of being adopted may be the real issue behind a child's questions or behaviors.

You might imagine a previously abused child should "forget" about his past experiences. If he tries to talk about them, you might discourage him. You may think it's best if you both pretend there wasn't any past for him. Instead, his life started the day you adopted him. This approach can be very harmful for a child, because his past needs to be accepted as real and valid, even if it was deplorable and horrible.

The best approach is a balance, one that accepts that the fact of being adopted may play a role in your child's life, but it doesn't necessarily affect everything.

By exploring the issues in this book, my hope is to help you create a balanced parenting approach.

The Risks of Parenting *Without* Common Sense

Of course no one means to abandon common sense, but sometimes we listen too much to others and not enough to our own knowledge of our child. In extreme cases, this can be dangerous. One adoptive mother didn't think she had developed a good attachment with an older child she had adopted. In apparent desperation, this mother contacted a therapy team in Colorado who recommended a "rebirthing" ceremony, in which the child would force her way out of the "womb"—actually some heavy blankets. This misguided idea ended tragically, with the child dying.

Obviously this went far beyond the minor mistakes that many of us make. I'm using this extreme example to illustrate that if someone offers you advice that's puzzling, bizarre, or illogical, and it would not be used in any other situation *except* adoption, you should be immediately suspicious and consult more trusted sources.

Common sense adoptive parenting is crucially important for your child. If you think Baby has colic because she was adopted, you may find yourself feeling too guilty and anxious to comfort your infant. If you think your older child is doing poorly in school because he was adopted, you may feel hopeless. You could take him to a therapist, but that might not help if the child is doing his best and his grades are still poor. The real problem may be a learning disability or a struggle with another child—both of which usually have nothing to do with being adopted.

Who We Are

The authors are Andrew Adesman, M.D., and Christine Adamec. I, Dr. Adesman, am a pediatrician with many years of experience in assisting and advising adoptive parents about health issues and problems of their children. The pronoun *I* refers to me throughout this book; however, my coauthor, Christine Adamec, has assisted me in writing the book.

I am the director of developmental and behavioral pediatrics at Schneider's Children's Hospital in New Hyde Park, New York. I am also an associate professor in the department of pediatrics at the Albert Einstein College of Medicine in Bronx, New York. In addition to being board certified as a general pediatrician, I am also board certified in developmental and behavioral pediatrics as well as in neurodevelopmental disabilities. I have written numerous articles and papers about adoption and other child development issues, both for medical doctors and for consumers. I speak frequently on adoption issues and other pediatric matters on television and radio media, and I have written articles for *Newsweek* and other publications. On a personal note, I am also the father of three healthy children.

Christine Adamec is a mother by adoption and by birth, and has written several books and scores of magazine articles dedicated to adoption.

Our Goals and Assumptions

We were inspired to write this book partly because of the "rebirthing" tragedy of the child in Colorado, and also because through the years we've heard many incidents of bad advice given to adoptive parents. We decided a common sense approach to adoptive parenting was needed.

We believe nearly all adoptive parents have the abilities and basic skills to be good parents. Our goal is to supply you with practical parenting information that you may not have heard before but that will, hopefully, make sense to you and help you become more confident in the advice you accept and in your own parenting abilities.

How to Use This Book

This book is divided into four parts. You may wish to read the book from cover to cover, or you may prefer to go right away to the sections that interest you most. Part I, which includes Chapters 1 through 5, covers the basics of common sense adoptive parenting, and common myths about adopted children and their parents. It also warns of problematic advice commonly given to adoptive parents and describes common parenting mistakes and how to avoid them.

Part II, Chapters 6 through 10, covers bonding and attachment, and then offers individual chapters on parenting infants and young children, school-age children, and adolescents. It also includes a chapter that discusses sibling issues, including the latest research.

Part III, Chapters 11 through 13, concentrates on explaining adoption to your child and others. It also offers sample conversations between adoptive parents and their children as well as conversations between adoptive parents and others.

Part IV, Chapters 14 through 16, covers special issues, including medical problems and disabilities your child may need help with, issues related to transracial and international adoptions, and what to do if your child has an emotional problem. Note: Children adopted at an older age are not separated out here, but rather information on children adopted from foster care, orphanages, or other arrangements is included throughout the book.

The Appendix discusses helpful resources, including information to help you locate adoptive parenting groups as well as print and Internet resources.

Note

All the names in this book of adoptive parents and their children have been changed to protect their privacy.

Part I

BASICS OF COMMON SENSE ADOPTIVE PARENTING

I

Common Sense
Adoptive Parenting

Adoptive parenting is a joyous and exciting job that sometimes brings extra challenges to you, your partner, and your child, as well as to other children you're raising. You need a healthy dose of common sense to travel down this path confidently.

All parents are subject to tons of advice, but with adoptive parenting it seems that the extremes are more prevalent. You are likely to hear a wide variety of ideas from social workers (some of whom may have little experience in parenting themselves), headlines that are geared more toward selling magazines and newspapers than to helping parents, and other sources. My goal is to help you sort through these ideas and eliminate any that are not commonsensical.

What Common Sense Is

What is common sense? It's that basic ability to think about possible courses of action, critically evaluate which choice seems the most logical, and consider the probable outcome. This may sound complicated, like learning how to play chess or speak Japanese. However, most people possess basic common sense, and it's a skill that can be honed. Of course, what constitutes common sense behavior isn't always crystal clear, which is why you need this book! Sometimes there are subtleties to navigate. My goal is to provide you with tactics to create your personal parenting game plan, incorporating common sense.

Along with thinking about whether particular actions actually make common sense or not, it's important to acknowledge the role of the "gut level" feeling. This is the feeling you get that says *No!* when other signs indicate something is probably okay. For example, your child wants to spend the night with a friend, you know the friend, and you may feel that you should give permission. But your basic instincts tell you something—you don't quite know what—is askew. In such situations, a little extra digging can usually elicit the information you need to make a common sense decision.

You may find out your child failed to mention that he and the friend planned to go on a camping trip in another city, and didn't expect you to ask any questions. Instead, they counted on you assuming the overnight visit was at the other child's house. But your gut level told you to probe further, and you didn't ignore it. Common sense parenting uses logical judgment combined with the basic parenting instincts that virtually all people have— whether your children were born to you or not.

Perceptions Versus Common Sense

If you're an adoptive parent, you may have already learned there are two key problems with adoptive parenting. One is how others perceive and treat adoptive parents and their children. You can't change what other people think, although there are many ways you can deal with the misperceptions of others, and I'll address those ways in this book.

The other problem lies in how adoptive parents perceive themselves. Sometimes, especially under stress, a parent may wonder if there is some truth in the many (mostly negative) ideas that others have about adoption. Don't fall into this trap. I'm not saying everything that others say about adoption is wrong. But often, it's suspect. Keep your skeptical mind in gear.

Why Common Sense Is Important for Your Child and for You

Sometimes adoptive parents are vulnerable to wrongheaded advice offered by some social workers and others. For example, one therapist advises parents that if their baby has colic, it's most likely due to the stress of separation from the birth mother.

Although there may be some changes in the baby's stress hormones that might exacerbate colic, it's unlikely that adoption is the sole cause of colic or most other physical problems that your baby may have.

Yet if you buy into the nonsensical belief that adopted babies with colic (or who are sick with other ailments) are ill solely because they were adopted, you may not make the best choices or may even create problems where none were present. Ironically, sometimes well-meaning parents, following the advice of social workers or other professionals and trying to do "the right thing," distress their children. One way they do this is by constantly reminding the child he or she was adopted.

For example, there are some wonderful children's books about adoption, and having one or two to read might be a good idea. But there's no need to buy nearly every children's adoption book and focus on those books to the exclusion of other wonderful works of children's literature. It's important to pay attention to what your individual child needs.

How Adopted Children Are Like and Unlike Other Children

Adopted children are like all other children. They need love tempered with discipline. They need interested parents who listen but who don't let them run the entire show. They need to feel safe.

Adopted children are also unlike other children. Most children don't have to face that they were not born to the people who are raising them. Sure, many kids have parents who are divorced, but most are living with at least one parent and can see the parent they're not living with, at least once in a while. A similar situation can occur in open adoptions, but there are still significant differences.

Society often expects both more and less of adopted children. People think adopted children should be grateful for being adopted and strive to do their best because they were "chosen." But they may also think that since the children were adopted, they can't achieve much. People may also think adopted kids are more prone to being neurotic than nonadopted children.

Accepting Differences and Similarities Is Important

Part of common sense parenting for adoptive parents is accepting the differences in their children. Just because you're great at art and your husband is a superb athlete, don't assume your child will be the same. You may also need to pursue new interests because they're important to your child.

At the same time, adoptive parents need to embrace similarities between themselves and their children. Why? Because it's important to seek common ground, as Lois Raynor found in her study of adopted children. This study is discussed in more detail in Chapter 3, but the basic premise is that children and parents need common ground. The happiest families are those who find some similarities among family members—even when no one else can see them. This doesn't imply differences are ignored. They are acknowledged and accepted.

It's important to try to see your child as she is, and not how you wish she were. Of course, you can have goals and desires for your child, and that's normal and even positive. But don't overlay a template of expectations on your child that can never work and will leave you both disappointed and unhappy. When you can see your child as she is, with flaws and talents and skills, you can be a far more effective and fulfilled parent.

Adoption as a New Beginning

Many new adoptive parents have concentrated so much time, energy, and sometimes most of their financial resources on adopting their child that they may think they're "done" once the child arrives in their home. At long last, the dream has been achieved. Success. The long adoption quest is finally over.

"When Lisa came home that first day, I thought to myself, at last! Now I can finally forget all that adoption and social worker stuff and we can get on with our lives!" said Anita, a new mother. But she quickly learned her life was changed, forever. Children have that effect on families!

Sometimes, even before you can spend much time reveling in the joy of having your infant or older child really, for sure *here*, the shock hits. This is hard work and it's not all kisses and hugs. When these feelings occur, many new adoptive parents are horrified, thinking they are unworthy, or have adopted the wrong child, or maybe they are not cut out to be adoptive parents at all. (Sometimes they think all these things.) Feeling overwhelmed, they beat themselves up mentally for having negative thoughts. They (and you) are not alone if they experience such emotions.

Overlaying the shock of new parenthood are the additional stresses and strains of being an adoptive parent. Sure, nearly everyone finds it a challenge to raise a child today. But many adoptive parents place heavy expectations upon themselves.

Some expectations are good, such as trying to be the best parent possible. Others are unreasonable, such as feeling you must be a perfect parent in order to deserve this child—especially if the birth family is still involved in any way. If you adopted a child with medical issues or an older child, you may feel you have to *prove* you can do this, to all those people who told you that you shouldn't adopt a child with any problems. You may feel compelled to show you really are Super Mom or Dad.

"It took us several years before we decided to adopt our baby," says Anne. "We wanted to adopt so intensely and it dominated our lives. But when Jenny came, the reality was not very much sleep, and hurried meals. Jenny was sick a lot at first, with ear infections." Anne wondered if she should ever have gotten herself into this, and then felt like a bad person for such thoughts.

Anne wasn't depressed, but was stressed and overworked. A key problem was that she was trying to do everything herself. Anne never hired babysitters or allowed family members to watch Jenny. "I raised *you*, didn't I?" said Anne's mother, offering help to Anne, but to no avail.

Anne thought since she was so blessed to have adopted her child, she had to be an extra-good parent. She also wanted to make it up to Jenny for the neglect she had suffered in the orphanage before she was adopted. But Anne was not really sure what "extra-good" was and was wearing herself out. Anne needed some downtime. She also needed to reconnect with her husband. They made love less, because what if the baby cried or needed something? Many opportunities for closeness were wasted because the baby did *not* wake up.

Happily, the blinders fell from Anne's eyes one day when she was reading a storybook to baby Jenny, who was sound asleep and quite oblivious. Anne longed to go out and have an adult conversation with someone, anyone. Before she slapped that thought down completely, she let it fully form in her mind. She decided yes, maybe it would be a good idea to do something other than baby stuff. That was the beginning of a balanced parenting approach for Anne.

Sensing What Children Need

One part of common sense adoptive parenting is using and trusting your senses to determine what your child needs. You listen (not just hear, but actually listen) to the child and observe.

You also notice if what is said doesn't mesh with what you see. The child who denies she broke the vase that you heard fall crashing to the floor while she was alone in the room is probably fibbing to you. Parents also learn to develop their gut instinct. Even if everything seems okay, sometimes something isn't right. In those cases, you ask more questions.

You also learn to look beyond the obvious, such as the shards of broken vase. For example, consider the example of Lori and her son Johnny, age eleven. Johnny was avidly interested in working to help people who suffered from the effects of an earthquake in Central America. His sixth-grade class was collecting blankets to send to earthquake victims, and Johnny wholeheartedly threw himself into this project.

Johnny's mother Lori and his teacher were delighted by Johnny's intense enthusiasm—but Lori suddenly had an insight. Maybe Johnny's efforts had something to do with the fact that he had been born in Nicaragua. Perhaps he feared his birth family was in danger and it was somehow his personal responsibility to provide assistance and relief.

Lori didn't assume she was right, because she wasn't sure. Nor did she take the direct approach, asking him if he was upset, because Johnny might not have realized it himself. Instead, Lori brought up the topic generally to see how he reacted.

Lori said to Johnny, "Sometimes children adopted from another country are really worried if a natural disaster hits that country. Sometimes they may think their birth relatives or children from an orphanage where they used to live could be seriously hurt and can be very upset about this." And then she waited. But not for long! Johnny burst into tears and told her how upset he was and how he felt guilty that he was safe and others from his birth country were not.

Lori gently told her son that a lot of people who have been adopted feel that way and it's understandable. She also told Johnny it was not his fault in any way that he was safe, while others were not. Of course, Johnny really did know he didn't cause the earthquake or harm the children. But he needed to hear it said. If Johnny had any "magical thinking" that he was somehow the cause, Lori relieved him of that notion.

Lori also told Johnny it's good to help others, reinforcing this core belief. Johnny continued his enthusiastic work but was less haunted and distressed after his talk with Lori.

What if Johnny had not become upset by what Lori said? Then she would have backed off the subject. She might have revisited it later if she sensed an underlying problem.

Key Elements of Common Sense Parenting

Common sense parenting is discussed throughout this book in a variety of scenarios and situations. To begin, let's examine several basic criteria for determining whether behavior (yours or that of others) is based on common sense. Ask yourself these questions:

1. Does my behavior or plan (or that of others) meet the basic common sense test: boiled down to its simplest level, could it work?

2. Is this behavior or plan born primarily out of fear or desperation? Or is there an underlying sense to what I'm considering? If it's from fear, it should be carefully thought out.

3. Would the average person think this behavior or plan makes sense? Sure, a lot of people don't understand adoption, but most people can grasp the basics. If an average person "on the street" would be dismayed by this behavior, rethink it.

4. Will the behavior or plan be harmful to the child? Many adoptive parents worry about every verbal misstep or parenting error, although in most cases, children are quite resilient. But sometimes, they aren't.

5. What are my primary motives (or the motives of others)? Do you want to anesthetize your child from comprehending the losses of adoption by either ignoring it or placing a great deal of emphasis on it? No parent can protect a child from all pain. This is a hard lesson for all parents to learn, but it's part of common sense parenting.

2

Debunking Common Myths About Adopted Children and Adoptive Parents

WHETHER YOU ADOPTED a baby or an older child, a child of the same race or ethnicity as you are or a different race or ethnicity, a child from your country or another country, a child who's healthy or with disabilities, a child who's related to you or one who's not, or a child from state foster care, an adoption agency, or adopted with the assistance of an attorney, it will probably shock you to learn that most of society and even most researchers lump all adopted children together into one category: adopted children. Then they make sweeping generalizations about this entire group.

It's like assuming all Asians or all women or all people older than age sixty-five think or act in one particular lockstep way. But when you realize there are about 1.5 million adopted children age eighteen and under in the United States according to the U.S. Census Bureau, and this number doesn't include adults who were adopted, it becomes even sillier to imagine them as people all alike in their behaviors and thinking. Yet such a generalization is presumed in the myths that adoptive parents and their children regularly hear.

The myths are especially painful when the accent is on something negative. If an adopted child exhibits problematic behavior (such as getting into trouble or doing poorly in school), some people (including some teachers) assume that this is just how "those adopted people" are.

Strangely, and looking at the other side of the coin, positive images are rarely generalized to all adopted people. For example, Wendy's International founder, the late Dave Thomas, and Olympic skater Scott Hamilton were both adopted as children, but few people conclude all adopted people make great businessmen or excellent ice-skaters. Nor should they make such assumptions! Adopted people are a very diverse group of individuals.

Because adopted individuals are often erroneously perceived as one homogeneous group of people, it's important for parents to understand the major myths about adoption perpetrated in our culture. With this knowledge, you can challenge such myths, when possible, or at least be aware of them when confronted with them, and you can prepare your child by explaining these myths.

I'll cover the myths that are most often heard, but of course there are other myths out there beyond the ones described in this chapter. Sometimes it may be hard for you to evaluate whether a generalization made about adopted children or a specific group of adopted kids (such as transracially adopted children or foster children who were adopted) is a valid one. For this reason, later in this chapter there are questions you can ask yourself to help you determine if such statements are likely to be mythical beasts rather than valid issues.

The Major Myths of Adoption

Here are some of the major myths about adopted children, adoptive parents, and birth parents.

Myth: Adopted Children Will Be Just Like Their Birth Parents

Adopted children receive their genetic attributes from their biological parents, such as their hair color, eye color, and general body type. The child may also inherit the potential for talents and skills, such as mechanical or artistic abilities, as well as some personality traits from their biological parents—such as a basically cheerful nature or a generally skeptical outlook. But few children are "just like" their biological parents. Even identical twins raised together have differences. A person's environment plays a role in making a person what he or she becomes.

A child may have similar interests to the parents she was born to. But she may also veer off into areas her biological parents never explored, such as music, dance, athletics, and so forth. Your job as a parent is to help your child identify and celebrate her best talents.

An insidious part of the "adopted children are always just like their birth parents" myth accentuates the negative aspects of a person. Rarely do people think about the *assets* of a birth parent. Instead, they think about the possible risks for developing alcoholism, drug abuse, or emotional disorders. This is sad, because some birth parents have problems, but they also have positive points too. One reason for the accent on the negative is that researchers are curious about social problems such as alcoholism, drug abuse, emotional problems, and so forth. They are far less interested in sobriety and mental wellness. Yet many studies also show that adopted children have virtually no greater risk for emotional disorders than nonadopted children. (Read Chapter 10 on a study of siblings.)

Myth: The Only Good Adoption Is an Open (or "Closed") Adoption

It's unclear to most people what an "open adoption" is, and social workers at different adoption agencies may define open adoption differently. Some agencies think a one-time meeting between prospective adoptive parents and a pregnant woman planning to place her baby for adoption is sufficiently "open" to qualify as an open adoption, even if a birth parent has no further contact with the adoptive parents or the child. Conversely, at some agencies, an open adoption is defined as one with frequent contact between the birth parents and the adopted child. How frequent may vary greatly. I define an open adoption as one in which the identities of the birth and adoptive families are known to each other, and if further contacts are made, it is a mutual decision.

However they define it, people who are in favor of open adoption are often *strongly* in favor of it, to the extent that they perceive "closed" adoption (confidential adoption) as harmful to the child. Interestingly, studies of children (notably by Harold Grotevant) in both open and confidential adoptions have revealed the children in both groups are well-adjusted.

Myth: Adopted Children Are Very Likely to Have Problems

"If someone commits a crime or gets into the news in a bad way, the media always makes a big deal if that person was adopted," says Chad, a teenager adopted as an infant. "Why do they do that? Are adopted people one of the groups that it's still okay to talk against?" Chad doesn't even like it when he reads a story about a movie star and his adopted children—he doesn't really understand why a person's adoptedness is mentioned at all.

Why is it important to say Miranda Starlet went to the premiere with her husband, her daughter, and her adopted son? Put another way, the media doesn't generally say Miranda went to the premiere with her husband and her biracial child by a previous marriage and her Hispanic adopted son. Only the "adopted" part is kept in.

What about the pathology part—do adopted children have more problems than nonadopted children? Some studies have shown adopted children are more likely to see mental health professionals than nonadopted children. In most cases, these studies fail to differentiate between children adopted as infants and children adopted from foster care after several years of abuse—they're all "adopted," and that's the only thing that appears to matter. It's unclear whether the child's problems stem from abuse or neglect that occurred before the adoption or from other issues.

Researchers have found that adoptive parents are more ready than nonadoptive parents to take their children to therapists, sometimes for relatively minor issues. (Read more about identifying and dealing with emotional problems if they do occur in Chapter 16.)

Some studies have shown many adopted children are well-adjusted. For example, in 1994, the Search Institute in Minnesota released the results of a study examining the outcomes for 881 adolescents adopted as infants and toddlers by families in the Midwest. The study revealed that by adolescence, the children were about as well-adjusted as the nonadopted children. In a few areas, such as knowing they were loved and identifying with their parents, they scored higher than adolescents born to families.

Myth: Adopted Children Are (or Should Be) Grateful

Should children be grateful because they were adopted, whether they were adopted from an orphanage, a hospital in Seattle, or someplace else? Some people think so. The reality, however, is that for most adopted children, their family is all they've ever known or can remember, and they have no other frame of reference. How could they be expected to be grateful for what's a normal life for them, as far as they know?

It would be nice if all children were at least a little grateful to their loving parents and the sacrifices made for them, but how many children do you know who think that way? There's no reason why adopted children should be expected to be especially grateful. If you're an adoptive parent looking for gratitude, you'll be disappointed, especially in your child's teen years. So don't buy into this myth!

What about the child with "special needs," for example, the child with physical or emotional disabilities who may have been placed for adoption because of those problems? Shouldn't a child with such problems be grateful he was adopted? Again, not really. I hope children love and respect the families who adopt them. I don't, however, think adopted children owe adoptive parents a special debt of gratitude, even when their birth circumstances or prior lives were dire. Parents make their own choices to adopt or not adopt children. Children live with the consequences of this decision, and hopefully this will result in mostly happy lives for them and their families.

Myth: Asian Children Are Always Good at Math and Science

Sadly, our society is still race-conscious, and if you adopt a child of another race or ethnicity from yours, people often notice and sometimes make stereotypical judgments about you and your child. For example, they may think your child must be extra-smart if she's Asian. Everyone *knows* Asian kids are great at math and science, right? This myth can be very difficult for the Asian child who's baffled by quadratic equations. (Read Chapter 15 for more information on racial issues.)

There are also some racist issues surrounding a child's country of birth. For example, people may say to a child that since he was born in Africa, his birth family must have died of AIDS. (This is a very intrusive comment to make, but sometimes people say such things.) Or they may state their presumption that children adopted from Russia must have come from an alcoholic family—another prejudicial remark.

Because of these ignorant stereotypes, it's important for parents to explain adoption to their children (as discussed in Chapter 11) as well as to discuss these stereotypical beliefs that some people cling to and have your responses ready.

Myth: Adoptive Parents Are Saints

Many adoptive parents are uneasy when told they're unusually wonderful people because they adopted a child. Some people who make such comments make the situation worse by adding they could never care for another man's (or woman's) child, a pretty hostile comment to make to an adoptive parent. Frankly, I think adoption *is* a good thing. But lots of people do good works. Adoptive parents are "regular" people and want to be seen as people with the same combination of faults and talents as anyone else. In addition, the problem with being perceived as saintly is that saints aren't allowed to complain about their children or ask others for help with problems that may come up. Who wants to be perfect all the time?

Myth: Adopting a Child Will Cause You to Get Pregnant

The myth that adopting a child somehow makes a woman get pregnant is still echoed throughout the United States. There was actually a study done by medical researcher Michael Bohman in 1970 on this subject, which he reported in his book *Adopted Children and Their Families*. Dr. Bohman found that about 8 percent of adoptive parents had a biological child later on. He discussed studies that showed postadoption pregnancy rates of from 3 to 10 percent.

Let's put this myth to rest: adopting a child doesn't make something magical happen so you or your partner will get pregnant. A pregnancy may happen if a person is still fertile. But usually it does not. And it's obviously not the reason you adopt a child—solely so that a woman will become pregnant. (Because if it *were* the reason, the chances of success are only about 10 percent, at best. Not very good odds.)

If a pregnancy does occur at some point after an adoption, people say annoying things, even in front of the adopted child. They say, "You should've waited, and you wouldn't have had to adopt a child." Or worse, "Now that you'll have one of your own, are you going to send the adopted one back?" It's hard to keep your temper when people make such remarks. But try. Count to ten if you need to. Then say you're very glad you adopted your child, and of course you are still your child's parent and always will be. Adoption is permanent.

Myth: Adoption Is Second Best to Having "Your Own" Child

This "second-best" myth, that adopted children are somehow not as good as children born to you, can really hurt you and your children. Some writers call it "adoptism," because it assumes adopted people are inherently inferior to nonadopted people. This is a bias, just as some people still think some races are inferior (racism) and some people still think women can't achieve as well as men can (sexism).

My coauthor Christine Adamec is a mother by birth and adoption, and she doesn't see adoption as second best—nor do any families she knows with both birth and adopted children. If someone tells you adoption isn't as good as having a biological child, ask the person how he or she could possibly know this, if he or she hasn't ever adopted a child.

Myth: Children Are Placed for Adoption Because There's Something Wrong with Them

Similar to the "second-best" societal myth is the myth that children are placed for adoption because there's something inherently wrong with them and basically, that their birth parents didn't want them because of this undesirable trait or set of traits. This is why some people may say such things as "If only her birth mother could see her now; she would never have given her up!" This statement is based on the premise that the birth mother chose adoption because the baby or child was somehow defective. The person is actually meaning to say something positive, but it is based on wrong and negative information. Statements like these should not go unchallenged.

Read the chapters on explaining adoption to understand how to deal with such comments.

Sometimes adopted children internalize this myth, believing that if they were smarter, more attractive, or in some way "better," the birth parents would not have chosen adoption. The reality is that in nearly all cases, the adoption choice was made because of a problem the birth parents had, and was not made because they didn't like the child. In fact, in most cases the adoption decision was made before the child was even born, so the birth parent couldn't even guess (based on birth appearance) what the child would ultimately look like or act like. In some cases, the adoption decision was made after the child was born, due to circumstances in the birth parent's life. In every case, including when the child was abused, neglected, or abandoned, the birth parent was unable to parent the child for whatever reason.

Myth: Good Adoptive Parents Always Have Happy Children

As a parent, your goal is to raise a happy and healthy child prepared to face challenges that lie ahead in adulthood. When there are problems (note I say *when*, not *if*, because eventually all children have some problems), you help your child resolve them as best you can. If it's a medical problem, you take the child to the doctor. If the child is having school problems, you consult with the teacher or maybe the principal. If the child suffers from emotional difficulties, you may need a good therapist. But no matter how effective you are as a parent, some problems simply crop up. They're not your fault or your child's fault. They just happen, and you deal with them.

Myth: Birth Parents Always Try to Take Away Adopted Children

If you believe what you see on some television shows (especially soap operas), birth mothers who choose adoption for their children always change their minds, and inevitably come to reclaim their children within months or even years later. Although there are a few court cases in which birth parents seek to regain custody, they represent a tiny minority of the thousands of adoptions that occur each year. However, the few cases that do occur are reported widely and can engender fear among adoptive parents and their children. In fact, some people are fearful to adopt children in the United States, assuming the myth of the birth mothers taking back their children is a reality.

In researching a reference book she wrote in 1999 (*The Adoption Option Complete Handbook*), my coauthor sent out questionnaires and received responses from hundreds of adoption agencies and adoption attorneys, and was startled by some of her findings. Most respondents reported few or no birth parents had changed their minds after the child was placed. One agency said, "In ten years, in four of 940 placements have children been returned to birth parents." Another said, "Of approximately 700 placements, there have been approximately 10 such cases."

As for the adoption attorneys, they too had few adoptions fall through after placements. The attorneys made such comments as "Less than 1 percent," "One, and that case is still pending and expecting a positive comment," and "In over one thousand adoptions, only five fall-throughs after the placement was made."

Yet the general public continues to believe many adoptions fall through, and some people may wonder out loud when the birth mother is going to show up on the adoptive family's doorstep demanding the child back. Tell them this almost never happens. (You should also reassure your child about the permanency of adoption.)

Myth: Birth Mothers Are Always Teenagers When Their Children Are Adopted

As myths go, this myth that all birth mothers are young teenagers is fairly benign. However, sometimes it's assumed the birth mother had no choice in the matter because she was a minor and her parents made her place the baby for adoption. The reality in the United States is that most teenagers under the age of eighteen who have unplanned pregnancies either get abortions or parent their babies themselves. If they continue the pregnancies, few adolescents have the emotional maturity needed to know adoption may be a good solution for themselves and their child. In addition, their peers in junior high or high school might condemn them for "giving up your own flesh and blood."

Most birth mothers who choose adoption in the United States are over age eighteen and are usually in their early twenties. Most are living apart from their parents, don't wish to go on public assistance, and don't have an ongoing relationship with the baby's father.

Little information is available on birth mothers in other countries. Some women in other countries who choose adoption or abandon their babies may be adolescents, but at least some of them are in their late teens or early twenties. They are usually not married, and raising a child in a nonmarital situation would be unthinkable in their culture. In some countries, such as China, where women may only have one child, married women may abandon a firstborn child if it is a girl, since boys are heavily favored over girls.

Myth: Adopted Adults Search for Birth Parents Because of Unhappiness with Adoptive Parents

The average American has seen television programs or read articles about both famous and average people searching for their birth parents. Many adoptees say that they search because they are curious about their birth parents, and many make a point of saying their adoptive parents are their "real parents." Yet the myth persists that adoptive parents whose children search for birth parents are cold and unloving people. It's unfair to assume that adoptive parents have somehow failed in their parenting if their children wish to search for their birth parents.

Myth: Adopted Adults Who *Don't* Search for Birth Parents Are Deficient

One myth purveyed by some adoptees devoted to search issues is that adopted adults who *don't* search are somehow defective individuals. Using a circular kind of reasoning, they convey their view that searching for birth parents is the normal path for adopted people, and thus, people who don't search are behaving abnormally or are "in denial" about their lack of desire to search.

The reality is very simple. Some adopted adults don't wish to seek out their birth parents and never do, and are happy with that position. Others do wish to locate their birth parents, and that's okay too.

It should also be kept in mind that not all birth parents wish to meet adults whom they placed for adoption as children, and in some cultures, an unmarried mother is still a cause for shame, as difficult as that is to believe in Western cultures today.

Myth: Older Children Adopted from Foster Care Don't Love or Miss Their Birth Parents (or Shouldn't, If They Do)

Many children adopted from foster care are school-age rather than infants or toddlers, and usually do remember birth relatives. (Although with the passage of the Adoption and Safe Families Act in 1997, many more children are being adopted from foster care at younger ages than in past years.) Sometimes birth relatives were abusive or neglectful. They may have used drugs or alcohol, left children alone for long periods, or completely abandoned them, among some reasons why children are placed in foster care.

Despite the abuse or neglect that may have occurred, most children have some love or affection for their parents or other relatives. These feelings shouldn't be denied. However, children need to hear from others, especially their adoptive parents, that the abuse was not their fault, because often children internalize guilt feelings.

Myth: Children Adopted from Foster Care Are Almost Always Permanently Damaged

Sometimes children adopted from foster care have or develop emotional problems. The myth is that *all* or most foster children who are adopted are doomed to unhappy lives. This is untrue. Some children have amazing resilience and can recover well from abuse, while others have a rocky road ahead of them.

What many people seem to forget, however, is what would happen to foster children if they were not adopted. They might be placed back with their parents, often to be abused again and reenter the foster care system. Alternatively, they might, as happens to many foster children, go from home to home. Before the passage of the Adoption and Safe Families Act, many children were in and out of foster care in a revolving-door type of experience until they "aged out" at eighteen, often completely unable to cope with life independently.

Adoption is a stabilizing experience for many foster children who would otherwise be "lost in the system," as one book title by Charlotte Lopez, a former foster child, put it. Lopez insisted on being adopted, and recounted her struggles in convincing state social workers that she needed a permanent family even though she was a teenager. She finally succeeded.

Myth: Adopted Children from Other Countries Can't Bond to Their Parents and Always Have Severe Developmental Delays

As discussed in Chapter 6 on bonding and attachment, most children and parents create an attachment to each other, and most studies of children from other countries (as well as children in the United States) indicate that children who are adopted under the age of three or four years old have the best chance of successfully bonding with their new families.

Some children have trouble bonding with their new families, as Chapter 6 states, although it can be hard to determine whether the underlying problem is one of needing time to respond to a new culture and new parents or if it's one of dealing with emotional conflicts based on the loss of everything the child has known, or other issues.

Coping with Stereotypical Statements

The following chart describes stereotypical statements that people sometimes make about adopted children, adoptive parents, and birth parents. It includes the statement itself as well as what adoptive parents often perceive as the underlying sentiment, and offers statements parents can use to defuse what was said. You can use the format of this chart to springboard you into thinking of other examples of stereotypical comments that people make, as well as how they make you feel and how you can respond in a neutral or positive way. (Screaming at the person who makes an offending comment is an understandable response, but it's not as effective as making a calm rejoinder—even if you have to count to ten first to get your temper under control so you can make a calm statement.)

Dealing with Stereotypical Comments

What Was Said	What You May Hear	Possible Comments to Make
You're a saint because you adopted.	You're extra good.	Thank you! Sometimes I worry my halo's slipping! *or:* I'm an average person who chose to adopt and am so glad that I did!
I'd never raise another man/woman's child.	Adopted children are bad.	I'm thrilled to be an adoptive parent and excited to help my child explore her abilities and talents as she/he grows up.
Adopted kids can have problems.	Adopted kids are trouble.	Sometimes kids, adopted or not, have problems. If they do, it's up to parents (like me) to help them.
Adopting a child always makes you get pregnant.	If you adopt, you'll get pregnant.	Really? And I thought sex had something to do with it! *or:* That's a myth. There have actually been studies that show this is not the case.
What if the "real mother" tries to take away your child?	The birth mother will take your child.	After children are with their adoptive families, birth parents almost never seek custody.

Evaluating Other Myths

It helps to be able to differentiate between myths and reality and stand up for your child when others perpetuate myths. How do you know if something is a myth? Here's a tool to help you. Ask yourself (or the person saying it) these questions:

- Where did you read about or hear this? (In most cases, the person can't remember. If the person remembers the source, you can investigate a little further.)
- Is there an organization making such statements? (If so, it may be a well-meaning group or one with a hidden negative agenda.)
- Does the statement sound like it could be plausible, or is it totally outlandish as far as you can determine?
- Would you believe a similar statement if it were said about another group of individuals, such as all blacks, all females, or all teachers? If not, perhaps a generalization that is made about adopted people could be a bigoted one too.

Consider the Source

Try to determine the source of the statement by asking the person who made the statement how he knows this. In some cases, it's just an urban myth passed around by people because it sounds interesting or shocking.

In the unlikely event that he does recall the source, don't be cowed into believing it if the statement was made by a politician or a researcher. They make mistakes too! However, in most cases, the possibly mythical statement was made by unknown people, and you can't trace it to a study or to an expert.

If you wish to investigate further, ask the reference librarian at your local library if she has information on this subject, which you think may be a myth rather than a factual statement. Do *not* ask the people at the front desk of the library who help people check out books. Ask the *reference* librarian. Reference librarians are trained to seek out information. In the age of the Internet, they can direct you to studies, newspaper articles, and many sources never available before.

Evaluate the Plausibility of the Statement

Think about whether the statement that you're unsure about seems to make sense to you. Also look for screening-out words like "always" or "all adopted children" or "never" or "no adopted children." These are usually red-flag phrases because they make generalizations about all adopted people. Rarely can valid generalizations be made about such a large and diverse group of people.

Consider Believability If It Were Applied to Another Group

Another way to evaluate whether a statement that is made about adopted children or adoptive parents or birth parents is to think if a similar statement would sound wrong or bigoted if applied to another group, such as all elderly people, all Hispanics, or another large group of individuals. For example, if someone told you most adopted children have attention deficit disorder, think about statements made about elderly people, such as that all older people have Alzheimer's disease. Only about 10 percent of all adults who are over age sixty-five in the United States have Alzheimer's disease. Of course, the risk increases with age, and 30 to 50 percent of people who are older than age 85 have Alzheimer's disease. Did you think the numbers were greater? Then you were buying into a popular ageist myth!

Another example: think about people saying that Hispanics are all hot-tempered. Is the "hot-tempered" comment a hasty generalization made about a large group of people? The answer is yes, it's an unfair generalization.

Use this tactic to help you differentiate between myths and realities in the statements that people make about adoption. Also, be sure to read Chapter 12 on explaining adoption to others, such as your parents, your child's teacher, your pediatrician, and other individuals. Even highly educated people can sometimes hold wrong ideas.

3

Problematic Adoption Advice

SOMETIMES IT MAY not be clear to you if the parenting advice you receive from others is valid or useful, regardless of whether it's offered by a person considered an expert or whether it's from family members, friends, or other adoptive parents. Experts (and your mom) may be right or wrong, but you need to use your basic common sense to help determine if the advice of others might be helpful before blindly following it. You also need to make parenting decisions based on what your child needs, not on how your parents reared you or even how other adoptive parents are raising their children.

This chapter examines frequently given bad advice imposed upon many adoptive parents, such as the advice that you should constantly remark on the many differences between you and your child without a similarly conscious effort to note similarities shared between you. Or advice that tells you if you don't think you and your newly adopted child are bonding well, you should force your child to act like a baby to bond with you. These examples of bad advice are countered by better parenting techniques you can try.

Experts Aren't Always Right

Many people assume what experts say must be correct because of their academic credentials or titles. But just because a social worker or a professor in a college who ran a study—or occasionally your own pediatrician—makes a pronouncement that something is true about adopted children, and, as a result, you should *always* do something or *never* do something else—doesn't mean this advice holds up in the real world.

Maintain a healthy skepticism, because sometimes the experts are off-target. This is especially true when they give one-size-fits-all advice generalized from a larger group to your child, such as all Russian children who supposedly act this way or all former foster children who supposedly do this or think that.

You deal with your child constantly, so you know him or her better than anyone else does. You need to make the best parenting decisions that you can, based on your child who's in front of you rather than on a textbook example child.

You might wonder, why should I believe the author of this book? He's an expert offering me advice, and maybe he's wrong too! Here's the difference. I provide a framework of general advice and strongly encourage you to use your own common sense, keeping your eyes and ears open as much as you can and considering the possible effects on your child.

You're *there* and I'm not. I can tell you about situations to watch out for and provide a variety of events that commonly occur with many children. But you must make the parenting choices, and hopefully, they're usually based on common sense.

It's also true that you can learn a great deal by listening to advice offered by others, and I don't want to dissuade you from opportunities to learn from experts and others. Cull out what works for you and your child and ignore the rest. That's what common sense parenting is all about.

Bad Advice: Emphasizing Differences Only

One bone I have to pick with some people who give adoption advice is a heavy emphasis accentuating *only* differences between adopted children and their parents, and their refusal to see a need to seek common ground between parent and child. This is yet another reason why constantly parroting "my beautiful adopted baby" is problematic: by chanting this phrase to your new infant, you concentrate on the differences between you, and you're the only one who notices them.

Here's some background for why some social workers and therapists accentuate the differences between adopted children and their parents. About a generation ago, in the 1970s and before then, nearly all adopted children were adopted by individuals of the same race, and many social workers also tried to "match" children by placing them with families that they looked like, so that no one would guess that the child was adopted. Adoptive parents were often advised that they should never tell their children they were adopted, and instead were told to pretend that the children were born to the family and to forget about the adoption. Sometimes adopted people found out they were adopted when they were age forty or older, and they were devastated to learn this secret.

In the late 1970s, people began adopting children of other races and ethnicities, making it hard or impossible to keep the fact of the adoption a secret. In addition, social workers and other experts began to realize that it really wasn't healthy for parents to ignore all the differences between them and their children. So adoption experts advised parents that they *should* tell their children that they were adopted, even when the child was of the same race or ethnicity as the parent was.

Social workers and other professionals involved in adoption also began to advise parents to emphasize the differences between them and the children they adopted. The social workers didn't offer this advice because they wanted adopted children to see themselves primarily as adopted and therefore different. Instead, these adoption advisors believed that *not* talking about adoption on a regular basis was a form of denial and consequently was negative, stigmatizing, and shameful. Conversely, they regarded frequent conversations and accentuating the differences of adoption as actions that were positive and nonjudgmental.

One problem that occurred was that some therapists and social workers overreacted and no longer advised parents to look for similarities between themselves and their children. Some of the people who advise adoptive parents began to perceive adoption as not simply a fact of life, but rather as the whole center of the child's life.

I believe that a balance is important, and this is why I think that parents need to consider both the differences and the real or apparent similarities between themselves and their children. I also think parents should tell their children that they were adopted, and because this is a difficult task for many parents, several chapters are devoted to this topic (Chapters 11 through 13).

A Better Way

Studies performed by Lois Raynor, an American social worker who lived in Britain, and described in her book *The Adopted Child Comes of Age* (National Institute Social Services Library, 1980), have confirmed that the happiest adult adopted children were those who thought they were similar in some ways to their adoptive parents (and whose adoptive parents also saw similarities with their children). This was true even when nobody else could see any similarities, and even when the adopted child was of another race or ethnicity. What mattered most were the perceptions of the parent and child. (Yes, this study is old, but it still stands up.)

This makes common sense. If you're constantly emphasizing how different your child is from you, your child is likely to start accentuating those differences in his mind too. "Yes, I'm *not* like Mom and Dad, we have nothing in common. I'm alien to them and they are to me."

Even good adoptive parents sometimes emphasize their differences with their children, at the expense of considering similarities. For example, if a coach says of your daughter, "She must have gotten her great running skills from you," many parents worry it would be inauthentic to say, "Yes, she gets it from me," since they don't share a genetic link with the child. But maybe you love running too, and you've been running together frequently and encouraging your child, so clearly there's a common interest.

You could respond to the comment from the coach by saying something like, "Yes, we both really love running!" It doesn't matter that it isn't a genetic thing—it's still a commonality you share, and you're not lying or misleading anyone by your statement.

And if you *hate* running? You could say, for example, "Not really, but Carly and I really like to swim together." (Some sporty activity, since you're talking to a coach.) Or you could smile and say nothing. The coach's comment, after all, was a rhetorical question, and nothing more. Don't make a huge issue out of it in your mind.

Identifying the Similarities

What if you feel like you're stuck in the differences mire and can't seem to see commonalities between you and your child? Maybe she's a sullen teenager and you don't *want* to see anything like yourself in her right now! It's still possible to work on finding common ground. I'm talking about actual common ground, and not pretending you really like rap music when you hate it, or saying you love clothes that you find hideous. Most children can tell when you're sincere. Also, if they're teenagers, they may *prefer* some items you'd dislike, as part of their distancing themselves from you and growing into their own identities.

The following questions may help you to find some of the similarities between yourself and your child.

1. Are you a "morning" or "night" kind of person, the kind who is happier and more alert at a specific type of day? What about your child? Your child may be like you in this respect. If he hasn't noticed it, point it out to him.

   Sometimes you'll be a morning person (a "lark") and your child may be an evening person (an "owl"), and that's okay too. You can still find other similarities.

2. Do you like specific types of foods that your child also likes, or share other preferences? You may share an attraction to anything chocolate or sweets in general. You can also find similarities in other preferences, whether in clothes (you both like to dress up or prefer casual wear) or hobbies (you both like fishing or bowling or other activities). When you start thinking about similarities between yourself and your child, you'll usually find them.

   Sometimes after a child has been in your family for years, you may think you know everything about him or her. But maybe you don't! You could make a game of it, in which you each separately list items such as "My favorite foods," "My favorite games," and then compare your lists.

3. Are you a tenacious kind of person who won't rest until you've gotten a job completely done? Or are you a start-one-job-and-then-move-on-to-the-next multitasking person? Think how your child older than three or four years old approaches tasks. Look for positive similarities or at least similarities you can commiserate on, such as you frequently losing your car keys and your child's constantly misplacing her skates!

    You don't need a genetic link to share personality traits with others. For example, if you're married or in a life relationship, your significant other may be extroverted and sociable, just like you are. Or perhaps he is serious and thoughtful, as you are.

    There are too many different personality traits to list them all here, but here are just a few examples of some personality traits and their polar opposites:
    - Impulsive/restrained
    - Quick to anger/slow to get mad
    - Excitable/calm
    - Active leader/happy follower
    - Generally optimistic/generally pessimistic

4. Do you have a spirit of adventure and like taking on new challenges? Or are you a more reticent and careful soul? What about your child? If you're both adventurous, maybe you and your child could enjoy boating trips together on your canoe or a rented boat. If that idea doesn't appeal to either of you, you may wish to go for a trip to the park to feed the ducks and have a relaxing picnic. If your child is adventurous but you're not, sometimes you need to get out there with him and do something you wouldn't normally do. Conversely, if your child is less adventurous than you, sometimes you need to encourage your child to try new activities, avoiding activities you already know your child hates.

5. Do you have a good sense of humor? Maybe your child has a different sense of humor than you have, but still sees humor in everyday events. Humor is often an effective antidote to difficult problems that occur in life, and it's a good trait for parents to encourage in their children.

Do you like the more subtle and ironic type of jokes or prefer quips or slapstick humor or silly sight gags? There are many types of humor that appeal to people, and your child may find hilarity in the same things that make you laugh. Of course, keep in mind that a child's sense of humor changes, and the fart jokes that are very funny to a ten-year-old boy will be much less hysterical to the same boy at the age of sixteen.

6. Do you share opinions about common experiences? Maybe you recall the third-grade field trip you went on together to collect insects was a total disaster because you spent the whole time knee-deep in mud in a mosquito-infested marsh. (Shared opinions can be things you like or detest. It's the "shared" part that matters.)

7. Do you have inadvertent similarities—even some that are humorous? Julia's eight-year-old son Michael professes to detest cats, although other family members like them. But every day, as he walks home from school, five neighborhood cats meet and greet him at their sidewalks. "I don't know why they love me!" Michael said, adding, "I guess if you're in my family, cats automatically love you."

Celebrate the Differences Too

While it's good to seek out similarities, this doesn't mean you shouldn't acknowledge differences between you and your child. In fact, an adopted child may have one advantage over the biological child, in that there's a lower probability you'll assume she *must* play the piano like you did, or he *must* go to business school like his father. Nonadopted children often chafe at these expectations, which may have been formed before they are even born.

With an adopted child, you can accept differences and even celebrate them. For example, you may be hopeless at physical activities, but your child's an athletic star. Or maybe you can't draw a straight line, but your child has artistic ability. Find differences that are admirable or that you can empathize with and talk about to your child in a positive way.

Many times, when people find differences between themselves and other people, they look at differences they don't like, such as the other person being messy or obsessively neat, or forgetful or rigid, and so forth. A better way is to identify differences you can admire. This doesn't mean you should start loving things that are repugnant to you, but instead it means that you seek out talents, interests, and abilities in your child that you personally don't have but you can encourage her to develop.

There are many different kinds of talents and abilities, but an alert parent can notice if, for example, a child is very manually adept. Other kids are knocking over their toy blocks but your Johnny has created a wonderful pyramid. Or your daughter has astonishing visual acuity and can see things you'd never see, even if you had special glasses. Maybe your child is very sociable, whereas you're more of a stay-at-home kind of person. If you look for differences that are positive, you will nearly always find them.

Bad Advice: Force a Child to Act Like a Baby to Bond

When a child is over age three when first adopted, she's had past experiences, many of which were probably bad (such as abuse and neglect) and some which may have been neutral or even positive, such as a relationship with a caring foster parent or a staff member of an orphanage. The child is not a blank slate at the age of three years old or older, and it's important to realize it may take time for you and your child to form an attachment to each other. (Read Chapter 6 for more on bonding and attachment and Chapter 11 for a discussion on explaining adoption to your child.)

How much time? It could be months or longer and will probably take more time than you would like. Some therapists have advised parents that their children will never bond to them unless they force the child to act like a baby. They think compelling a child to exhibit such behavior will speed up the bonding process. This idea may be appealing to some parents, who don't want to wait a long time for their children to become attached to them. Sadly, the shortcuts suggested by some people are dangerous, while others are not helpful and may be inappropriate.

There are several examples of behaviors that I don't recommend, such as forcing a small child to use a bottle and punishing her if she wants to drink out of a cup. Or forcing the walking child to crawl instead of walk. If a child wants to drink from a bottle or is open to the idea of crawling, that is one thing. But to compel a child to act like an infant, after her repeated attempts to behave in an age-appropriate manner, can be emotionally or physically abusive behavior. Rather than bringing parents closer to the child, it can drive them apart.

Another example of bad advice is to hold a child tightly on your lap and refuse to let her go. Of course, sometimes you *must* hold onto wiggling children, to change their diapers when they're little or to bathe and dress them. And you must also protect your child from danger. But to compel a child over the age of three years to stay on your lap, held very tightly and for a prolonged period, may be considered excessive.

Some social workers have advised parents that in order to bond with their infant or child they must force the child to stare at them, and should hold the child's head so she will be forced to comply. Staring contests when one person (you) has all the power don't make for good attachments. In some cultures, in fact, it is considered disrespectful for a child to look into an adult's eyes.

Instead, if your child has trouble looking at you, you could try other gentler methods. You can gradually teach your child to look at you by saying things like, "You can have the toy right after you look at me." Then when the child responds by looking straight at you, if only briefly, give him the toy. Gradually, you can build up the time that a child will feel comfortable looking at you. But don't throw your own adult temper tantrum if sometimes the child forgoes the toy because he doesn't feel like looking at you. A good pediatrician or therapist will be able to offer other behavioral suggestions or insights. For example, occasionally poor eye contact may indicate the presence of a developmental disorder.

If a therapist or another person insists the parental behaviors I have advised against in this chapter are ones you *should* institute, ask him why and listen to the response you get. Use your common sense, saying no to the therapist when no is the right answer to give. Parenting isn't easy work! You're your child's advocate and need to do what's best for your child. If that conflicts with what a therapist or another person wants you to do, consider seeking a second opinion before following or dismissing that advice.

Bad Advice: All Good Adoptions Are Open

Another mistaken idea is that open adoption is the only path to happiness for an adopted child. In fact, some people who adopted their children in open adoptions may be told their adoption isn't open "enough," and they should have *more* contact with the birth parents. I think you should do what's best for your child, realizing open adoptions can be very workable, but are not always ideal.

I am not against open adoption at all, but simply believe that there are different ways to have a successful adoption. The belief that only one type of adoption is a "good" adoption is a myth refuted in Chapter 2. Many open adoptions are happy and successful, so if you adopted your child in an open adoption, everything should work out well in most cases. But conversely, if you adopted your child in a confidential adoption, you have no reason to feel guilty, because most children adopted in a confidential adoption are also happy. There is no path that is right for everyone.

Don't listen to others who insist you must immediately take steps to open the adoption to avoid catastrophic consequences that may occur later on. In fact, acting hastily sometimes may lead to disastrous results, especially if your child is going through the tumultuous teens.

Think about it. It can be difficult to locate birth parents, and sometimes it's impossible, especially if they live in another country. If they are identified and located, the birth parents are not always receptive to meetings. They may be experiencing difficult problems themselves, with their other children or with whatever life has thrown at them. It's by no means an obvious undertaking that you should open a confidential adoption, unless you believe that you have a compelling reason to do so.

The impact on your child should be considered, keeping in mind that the outcome is highly unpredictable. Kerry, a mom who opened her daughter Mindy's adoption when Mindy was thirteen, now regrets it. The birth mother, Lisa, didn't cause a problem, and Kerry thinks she's very nice. But

Lisa's other daughter Eva, Mindy's biological sister, was seventeen when the two teens met. She *did* cause a problem.

Eva smokes, drinks, and is sexually active. She's had a negative impact on Mindy, who has tried to emulate Eva's bad behaviors. Of course, Mindy might have acted out on her own anyway, had she never met Eva. But some preliminary study results indicate children copy negative behaviors of their older siblings, whether adopted or not. (Read Chapter 10 for more information.)

It's also true that the outcome to opening an adoption may be very favorable. The key is accepting ahead of time that the results will be unpredictable.

Bad Advice: Adopted Kids Always Need Therapy

Some adoptive parents are told that they should, at the slightest hint of trouble, rush their child to a therapist. In fact, some people think nearly all adopted children need therapy, even if they don't show any obvious signs of trouble. It's certainly true some adopted children can benefit from therapy, particularly if you adopted them as older children, and sometimes even when they were adopted as newborns. But racing your child off to see a psychologist at the slightest sign of trouble is a bad idea. It can sometimes create problems that weren't there in the first place.

In a 1994 article in the *Journal of the American Academy of Child and Adolescent Psychiatry*, psychiatrist Steven Nickman and social worker Robert Ewis said some therapists don't treat children who were adopted as infants as a different group from children who were adopted as older children. In addition, some therapists may not appreciate the strong bond between a parent and a child when the bond was created by adoption. Nickman also reported that therapists sometimes shut out adoptive parents and are only willing to see a child alone.

Don't rule out help when needed, but be very judicious in taking your child to a therapist and be careful in selecting the therapist. Your child's pediatrician may be helpful in identifying appropriate therapists or resources in your community. Read Chapter 16 for more information on therapy and therapists.

Bad Advice: Lots of Love Now Cancels Out All Past Problems

Some experts imply—and some parents think this on their own—that if you love your child enough and provide him with everything he needs to grow up happy, any negative effects of the preadoptive environment will be erased, no matter how bad the earlier environment was.

Sadly, it isn't true that love wipes out the effects of all past problems. Although many children are amazingly resilient, and with help can largely overcome the effects of severe abuse and neglect in early life, the impact cannot be completely eradicated by a loving family. Parental love can help ease the pain, but it doesn't make it magically disappear.

Sometimes there isn't much pain from the past for your child because you adopted him or her as an infant. It's true that your child may be sad about being adopted sometimes, but when that happens, it's not because you failed your child by not loving him or her well enough.

It's tough for most parents to accept this, but your child will face some difficult experiences in the course of life. We parents can't insulate our children from all the troubles and emotional pain that will occur, as much as we wish we could. Our love can somewhat cushion life's slings and arrows. But there will still be some major stings along the way, no matter how much you'd like to take all the pain on yourself.

Sorting Out Advice from Your Family and Friends

Often it's not experts who give the problematic advice, but well-intentioned family members or friends. Again, you must figure out what's best for your child. Even preschoolers can understand rules and be expected to follow them, and know the basic difference between good and bad behavior. But tailor the consequence or reward to the child and the situation.

Your parents, siblings, and friends may recommend that bad behavior at the dinner table should mean that a child is sent to bed without dinner or at least without dessert. But let's say you've recently adopted your child from another country, where she never knew where her next meal was coming from. Withholding food from such a child can be perceived as an egregious punishment. This doesn't mean you never punish children adopted from other countries or from poor circumstances in your own country. The key is to keep in mind your child's frame of reference when you create punishments to correct his or her behaviors.

Your family and friends may urge you to spank your child for misbehavior, but in general, noncorporal punishments work best, and spanking should not be the routine, primary form of punishment for any child.

Don't Worry About Spoiling the Child (Unless You Are!)

What of the claims of others that you're "spoiling" the child if you don't follow their advice? In the case of the child who had been starved, you could tell others your child suffered from malnutrition in the past, and withholding food is an inappropriately severe punishment for her—if you wish to tell them anything. (You're in charge, and don't have to explain everything you do to others.) Or tell them you're doing what's right for your child, and leave it at that. Keep in mind that most nutritionists and psychologists now say it's best to avoid using food as a punishment or a reward, because it may set up an unhealthy emotional attitude toward eating.

If the advice does seem to hit home, think about it. Sometimes others are right that you're giving in to your child too much. However, it's still up to you to decide the right balance. If you're uncertain, your child's pediatrician may be a helpful resource.

Make a List of House Rules

It can help both you and your child if you make a list of your basic rules and routines, as well as the consequences you've devised for when the rules are broken. Keep in mind that you should use rewards as motivators whenever possible rather than punishments. When you do use punishments, they are most effective when they are immediate. Saying that a child won't be able to do a valued activity this weekend does not have the same impact as giving a consequence right away.

When the child breaks one of your rules, in addition to giving your child a consequence, make a mental note of the rule violation. Later on, review what happened. You may decide that the rule was too difficult for the child to follow or that a consequence was too lax or severe.

In addition, if you've just adopted an older child, it may be a good idea to show your basic list of rules to your pediatrician and/or other experienced parents. Sometimes parents have unrealistic ideas of what a child can achieve at a particular developmental level, and the insights of others can help you adjust your parenting course, if needed.

Make sure also that when others (including family members!) will babysit your child, you tell them not to withhold food or to use other punishments you disapprove of. Let them know what your house rules are, and how you usually enforce them. In addition, emphasize to all babysitters what specific behaviors you frown upon from them, such as smoking around children or yelling harshly.

Bad Advice: Emphasize the Losses of Adoption

Some feel that parents should be sure to educate their children about adoption losses, such as the loss of the biological mother. This is bad advice for many reasons. One common sense reason why it's bad advice is that if you emphasize the negative, that's what the child will see as most important. Of course if the child feels sad about being adopted and wonders about her birth parents, it's important to acknowledge those feelings. Such emotions may come on their own, and if they do, you can agree with your child that it's sad everyone can't grow up with their birth parents, even though you're happy that you were able to adopt the child.

Questioning Prebirth Losses

Watch out for people who tell you that children adopted as babies are sad or distraught because they miss their birth mother, whom they connected with during pregnancy. There is no evidence this is true, and it is a manifestation of a belief set only. Most adults can't remember what happened to them before they were three or four years old (other than possible severely traumatic events), and there's no reason to believe children, adopted or not, can remember what it felt like to be in the uterus, and consequently may be sad because the person with that uterus is not in their lives.

Again, this is not to deny the sadness adopted children sometimes feel because they know they were adopted and wonder why it happened. (Read Chapter 11 on explaining adoption to your child.) That's a real sadness. It's just not based on a fetal memory, as far as anyone can tell.

Thinking About Gains

It's a bad idea to accentuate the losses of adoption at the expense of gains that your child has obtained with your family. For example, the child now has a family (your family) who really wanted her, and she usually has a good life. There are also many intangible benefits. For example, in one unique study reported in a 1999 issue of the *Proceedings of the National Academy of Sciences*, researchers Michel Duyme and colleagues looked at sixty-five children in France adopted after the age of four years, and who had intelligence quotients of less than 86 when they were adopted. (An IQ of 100 is normal.)

The researchers found being adopted boosted the children's intelligence scores when retested in adolescence by an average of 14 points. This means some children who were "slow" were subsequently able to develop normal intelligence levels in their adoptive families.

Adoptive parents aren't perfect people who provide perfect homes. But in most cases, there are plenty of gains to adoption, and it's a good idea to tell your child about these pluses too.

Sorting Out Good Advice from Bad

Sometimes it's confusing to sort out advice from others. In some cases, you may not know if advice will work for your child unless you actually try it. In other cases, it's apparent the advice is not something you'd wish to try. In differentiating advice others offer you, ask yourself these questions:

- Who's the source? Your mother, a stranger, or someone else? (Do you trust the source?)
- Does this advice seem to make sense?
- Could following the advice be harmful?

- Would your pediatrician approve of this advice?
- What are your child's needs? (This advice might work for some children, but be disastrous with your child.)
- Is this advice part of a parenting competition? (My child got potty trained before your child, so I win!)
- Are you relying on behavioral or developmental norms that may not apply to your child? (A child adopted from an orphanage at the age of two is generally not going to weigh the same as a child raised in the United States from birth by her family, nor will she be on track developmentally right away.)

Consider the Source

When you're offered parenting advice for your child, think about who's giving the advice. Is it someone who's never had children? Often, adults who don't have children are convinced they'd *never* have a child who would scream for a toy or candy. They'll find out, if they ever become parents, that children are often messy and cranky. For now, don't worry about what they think.

If the advice comes from your mother or a brother or sister with children, it might be useful, but be sure to ask yourself the other questions in this section as well. Also, keep in mind that the circumstances in which you or a nephew or niece were raised were usually very different from what your child has experienced. You and they probably were not adopted from a foster home or orphanage. Even if you were, the circumstances now would be different from what occurred when you were a child.

Is the Advice Sensible?

Another question to ask yourself is if the advice is sensible. If someone tells you to spank your two-year-old child for misbehavior, this is not good advice. Two-year-olds don't know the difference between right or wrong because they haven't developed a moral compass yet. They can't really be "bad."

Spanking isn't effective in most older children either. Effective limit-setting can be established and reinforced using behavioral techniques without relying upon physical punishment. Consider using time-outs as consequences, if appropriate for your child.

Parent: Do No Harm

You need to discipline your child as she grows and to say no periodically to your child. But avoid following advice that might harm your child. For example, don't teach your child to avoid hot water by sticking her hand under scalding water: that's abusive.

What Would Your Pediatrician Think?

Another way to consider whether advice on parenting children would work is to think what your child's pediatrician would say. If you imagine describing the advice to your doctor, and the first image that comes to mind is your doctor's shocked expression, it isn't advice you should follow. If you're not sure if the advice is useful, then ask the doctor. If it's not an emergency, call the office and leave a message, and the physician or nurse will get back to you later on.

Think About Your Child's Needs

It's important to consider your child as an individual. If Grandma says you should let your baby sleep in total darkness but Baby is afraid of the dark, ignore Grandma and get a night-light. You could also leave all the lights on, working on gradually dimming them over several nights, giving Baby time to adapt to less (but not no) light.

If you adopted a toddler from an orphanage in another country and your new child, age three, isn't potty trained yet, don't panic. Give her time to adjust to your family and slowly introduce potty training concepts. She has a lot to get used to, such as a new family, new language, and a whole new culture.

Don't Compete with Other Parents

Many parents compare notes with other parents, and then feel bad if their children aren't "performing" as well as other children. If a parent brags little Tiffany was talking, walking, and doing somersaults (I'm kidding about the somersaults) at one year old, other parents may feel their children are backwards if they haven't mastered these skills. They may worry it's their fault, and even get into a panicked state.

Parental competition can be especially problematic if you adopt a child when she is a toddler from foster care or an orphanage, where she may have received inadequate stimulation and poor care. Your child needs time to catch up from initial deprivation.

When other parents play the "My child is better than yours" game, stay out. If others insist on asking about milestones your child has achieved, tell them your child is on track. (You don't have to tell them it's the three-year-old-just-adopted-from-China track.)

If you wish to tell others your child was adopted and needs time to adjust to his new family, that's fine. But don't feel compelled to share this information with every parent in the park, to excuse the fact that your child is not sprinting alongside their children. Also, if *your* child is ahead of other children, please refrain from bragging and making the other parents feel inferior!

4

Examining and Dealing with Expectations

YOUR PERCEPTIONS AND the perceptions of others affect your child. What do you think of adopted children in general, and your child's adoption in particular? This chapter covers the importance of your own expectations for your child, and provides a self-test of your expectations and what your answers may mean. It also discusses how to deal with the expectations others have of your child.

Consider Your Expectations for Your Child

All parents have expectations and hopes for their children. Some people are more detailed in their expectations than others. All good parents hope their children will be happy and healthy. Beyond that, parents diverge quite a bit.

There are many problems with overly high or excessively low expectations. If you expect your child will become a clone of you, you're bound to be disappointed. This is an expectation that biological parents often have, but adoptive parents can sometimes fall into this trap too.

Tender loving care and a good education can certainly help, but there's also an upper-limit ceiling that we all bump up against. In addition, the child may have very different interests from yours, and may prefer to be a teacher or an artist rather than a leader of industry or a corporate attorney.

Don't shortchange your child by assuming he can't do anything either. Give children the chance to fail at tasks that other children their age can perform. Children learn from mistakes as well as from achievements. The trick is determining where the ceiling is, and not overestimating (or underestimating) what your child is capable of.

Be observant about what your child appears good at. Teachers, relatives, and others can help you notice your child's talents. And be adaptable and ready to change your evaluation. For example, Sandy thought since her teenage son Todd never liked to read much (although he could read), he'd have to take a low-paying job when he grew up. But Todd developed an interest in cars and devoured auto mechanics manuals that were impossible for Sandy to understand. Sandy realized Todd might make a good mechanic or maybe an engineer. She kept an open mind and talked to Todd about careers, as did his guidance counselor. Todd decided to become an auto repair mechanic and was very successful and happy in this career choice.

Expectations may vary for how children will behave as well as how children will develop into adults. For example, some people expect their children to be very well-behaved and don't want to hear any yelling. It's possible to have a quiet household, depending on how you act yourself and what you reinforce in your child. Other people think children should be active, expressive, and opinionated and would view a quiet and sedate child as odd.

As for expectations for adult children, some people are happy with whatever the child can achieve. Others aren't happy unless their child is a college graduate and is employed in a professional field, preferably one similar to their own.

Your expectations will drive how you parent your child now. For example, when the child's behavior deviates from however you define "good," you'll admonish the child. And if you consider it imperative that your child go to college, you'll press him to do well all through school so he can be accepted into a college.

The problem comes when you expect behavior that's difficult or impossible for your child to comply with. For example, if you want a quiet child, but you've adopted a hyperactive child, your child will rarely be able to meet your expectations. If you've adopted a child with average intelligence, but you expect she'll grow up to be an aeronautical engineer, your child probably won't be able to meet that goal either.

Another problem comes in determining what your child is capable of. For example, a hyperactive little boy doesn't bounce off ceilings twenty-four hours a day. Most children, including very active ones, can be quiet when engaged in activities they find fascinating. Part of your job as a parent is to try out different activities to discover which are most appealing to your child.

Your child may also be brighter (or less bright) than you or his teachers realize. He may have a learning disability, which may be misinterpreted as low intelligence by teachers and others. Or he may be functioning at his best and not have any learning disabilities. Sorting this out can be a daunting task. (Read more about talking to teachers, doctors, and others in Chapter 12.)

Keep in mind that if you've recently adopted your preschooler child from an institutional setting, don't rush to judge her long-term potential based on initial impressions. Although assessment for possible remedial services would be appropriate in many cases, don't assume that a child newly adopted from an orphanage is exhibiting her long-term and best potential.

If you (or others) misjudge a child as average when she is in fact very bright, your child could miss out on opportunities. Other people may see her as the "poor little adopted child, we can't expect much from her." As a parent, it's your job to help your child stretch to her full abilities—without breaking her in the process.

Take the following simple test to help you zero in on your expectations for your child. Then compare your answers to how your child is doing. If there seems to be a mismatch, maybe you should rethink your expectations. And remember, it's just as serious a mistake to have overly *low* expectations as to have excessively high ones.

There are no right or wrong answers in this test; it merely explores your expectations for your child. It may also help you help your child achieve these goals. If you have more than one child, take the test separately for each child, because most parents have different expectations for different children.

Expectations of Your Child Self-Test

	True	False
1. My child should graduate from high school.	☐	☐
2. My child should graduate from college.	☐	☐
3. My child should grow up to be self-supporting.	☐	☐
4. My children (if you have more than one child) should be friends with each other.	☐	☐
5. I want my child to see me as his/her advocate.	☐	☐
6. My child might need therapy because of the adoption.	☐	☐
7. My child should receive good grades (As and Bs).	☐	☐
8. My child should make a contribution to society.	☐	☐
9. My child should be religious.	☐	☐
10. My child should have friends.	☐	☐
11. My child should grow up to be responsible (have a job, pay taxes).	☐	☐
12. My child should be a loving person.	☐	☐
13. My child should love animals.	☐	☐
14. My child should be athletic.	☐	☐
15. My child should be artistic.	☐	☐

Now, consider your answers. If you answered "true" to questions about your child graduating from high school and college and getting good grades (questions 1, 2, and 7), education is important to you, and you'll need to take your child's educational abilities into account. You should also play an active role in your child's education. You should meet with your child's teachers on a regular basis (whether she gets good grades or not) and, if possible, do some volunteer work at the school.

If you're unhappy with the education your child is receiving, work with your local district staff about your concerns and explore what options there are. If this proves unsuccessful, you can then investigate other alternatives, such as charter schools (schools that receive public money but concentrate on children with specific needs or interests), private schools, or you may wish to consider homeschooling your child.

Next, if you answered "true" to questions 4, 10, and 12, your child's sociability is important to you. Keep in mind that some children are more introverted than others, and the bookish child usually isn't going to be prom queen. (Although it sometimes works out that way.) Still, it's important for children to have friends, and it's good to be a loving person.

Watch out about expecting your children to all love each other. Sibling rivalry rears its ugly head in the best of families. (Read more about siblings in Chapter 10.)

In question 5, you want your child to see you as her advocate, and most of the time, that'll happen. However, when your child starts lurching into adolescence, you're far more likely to be regarded as "Them" than as an "Us" person by your teenager. This isn't necessarily an adoption issue, although adopted teenagers may think to themselves they're glad they're not genetically related to such a hopeless person. (Things usually get better: the child becomes an adult, and you become much less stupid—according to your child—than you were before.)

In question 6, if you think your child is likely to need therapy solely because he or she was adopted, this could be a problem. It's good to be aware of the possible need for therapy, but don't assume all adopted children need therapy. Read Chapter 16 about emotional problems.

Questions 3 and 11 are questions about personal responsibility. If you want your child to grow up to be self-supporting, this is often (but not always) a reasonable expectation. You may wish to pursue this goal by teaching your teenager how to balance a checkbook or talking about things like income taxes and tax deductions.

Questions 8 and 9, about wishing your child to grow up and make a contribution to society and to be religious, may be important to you. If so, show your child it's important to contribute to society by doing volunteer work yourself and making a public or lasting contribution. Take your child along. If you want religion to play a role in your child's life, take him to religious services with you. However, understand that even the most devout parent may have a child who's uninterested in religion.

The last three expectations are specific, including wanting a child to love animals, be athletic, and be artistic. If you're an animal lover, you probably have pets. Teach your child to take care of the cat or dog, and take the child with you to the vet when the animal has checkups. If you want to encourage an interest in the arts, take the child to museums, plays, and other cultural opportunities. Your child may be incapable of drawing a straight line, but able to appreciate and enjoy music and art.

As for athletics, many children aren't going to grow up to be great at team sports, but can take advantage of biking, swimming, and other activities. Encourage them to do so, and participate in these activities with your children.

If you have other expectations you think are important, write them down on a sheet of paper. Then think about whether these expectations are achievable by your child, and if so, what you can do to help your child achieve them.

What Others Expect from Your Child

You're not the only person who has expectations of your child. If you have a partner, he or she will have expectations that may be similar to yours. (Hopefully, they won't be completely opposite.) Your child's grandparents may also have expectations, which may be reasonable or not. For example, if they mistakenly remember you as an obedient child (having forgotten the many times you annoyed them), they may expect your child to be an obedient child too. And if he isn't, they may blame that on the child's being adopted. It could also be useful if your spouse or partner takes the self-test earlier in this chapter, using it as a focal point for discussion between you.

The child will also face the expectations of teachers. Some studies have indicated that when teachers find out children were adopted (with the possible exception of Asian children, who are often assumed to be very bright), they go easier on them than other students. This can mean the child may not be sufficiently challenged in school.

You can't easily change the expectations others have of your child—if you can change them at all. But sometimes you can point out that these expectations aren't working for your child. If Grandpa says Tommy is acting up, unlike his father, you could remind him of times he told you about in the past when Tommy's father misbehaved. You should be able to find relatively minor examples, such as when Grandpa found out his son cut school to go fishing and came home covered with mosquito bites and a nasty sunburn.

In this way, Tommy is a "chip off the old block" if he misbehaves, but not so bad that Grandpa may think negatively about Tommy (or about his own son!).

Children also have their own self-expectations. For example, Julie's mother overheard Julie (who was adopted as an infant) announce to a friend that of course she'd be going to college, because everyone in Julie's family goes to college. No one had ever told Julie she was expected to go to college or had to go. She had incorporated this perceived expectation on her own.

5

Common Parenting Mistakes and How to Avoid Them

MANY PEOPLE FALL into the common trap of thinking that if they try really hard to be good parents, they'll make few (or no) mistakes. If you're a parent with this view, you're in for a rude awakening, because you *will* ultimately make some errors. It's not because you're an adoptive parent. It's because you're a *parent*. All parents make plenty of mistakes, and it's important to realize this, try to prevent making them when you can, and avoid repeating the mistakes you do make.

No matter how effective and loving a parent you are, or how careful, discerning, smart, or well-educated, you're still human. Sometimes you won't have all the facts, and you'll blunder. Maybe you'll accuse your child of doing something wrong, but it really *was* the dog that ate the cookies. Or maybe you'll be overtired or ill and make an error. Yelling is one of the best examples of ways in which frustrated parents sometimes (and often, for some) engage in an unnecessary behavior that children will copy.

This chapter isn't about transforming you into a perfect parent. Instead, it's about helping you know about, and hopefully avoid, common mistakes many other parents have made. Knowledge is power.

Sometimes parents agonize over their parenting mistakes, not realizing nearly every day is a new chance to do a good job, and most children are forgiving. As long as you're caring and attentive—and you're not abusive or neglectful—you're probably doing a good job. An abusive parent hurts a child in many different ways. A neglectful parent doesn't provide food, clothing, or shelter, or doesn't protect a child from others who are abusive.

This chapter talks about common parenting errors from two perspectives. First, there's your own perspective, and I describe the type of parenting challenges many parents face, but which often seem to be traps for adoptive parents, such as overindulging a child, not knowing how and when to apologize to your child, not enforcing your own privacy/boundaries, failing to obtain needed immunizations, and not acknowledging your child's feelings.

This is followed by a second perspective, specific behavioral problems many (but not all) adopted children exhibit, such as problems with eating and sleeping, and suggested ways to deal with these problems. (School problems are addressed in Chapter 8 and sibling issues in Chapter 10.)

Overindulgence: The Most Common Parenting Error

If I had to fault adoptive parents for any one general flaw, it's overindulging their children—although many nonadoptive parents fall into this pattern as well. Others call it "spoiling" a child. I'm talking about parents who not only strive mightily to please their child, but who often attempt to anticipate the child's every whim before it takes shape in her mind. You've waited such a long time and wanted a child so much that when your child is finally in your home, you may fall into the overindulgence trap. This isn't good for you or your child.

Overindulgence can come in many forms. It can loom up in the form of buying your child everything he expresses a passing interest in. It can come in the form of rarely (or never!) saying the word *no*. It can also derive from your attempts to make everything easy, sort of the opposite of "no pain, no gain." In the overindulged child's case, he gains whether he endures minimal emotional pain or not. This is not good preparation for the cold outside world that lies beyond your family, a world your child will eventually have to cope with, even as early as kindergarten or preschool.

You do not have to run your family like you're the drill sergeant and your children are your little soldiers. Nor should you act like Scrooge (before he understood the true meaning of Christmas) and withhold your time, gifts, and love from your child. Just don't overdo it.

How do you know if you fall on the overindulgent side? Take the self-test later in this section to find out.

If You Think Too Much Isn't Enough

When you've wanted a child for a long time, maybe years, and at long last you've adopted, you may want your child to have everything. Maybe your desire to overindulge your child stems from a giving desire run amok. Or perhaps you are trying to atone for the fact that your child was adopted or for bad things that occurred (or may have occurred) in the past.

Don't make this mistake. You can't (and shouldn't try to) make it up to your child for his hard life before he was adopted by overindulging him with material possessions. Or, if he was adopted as a baby and *hasn't* had a hard life, you can't make it up to him for being adopted rather than being born to you. All the treasures in the world can't change the adoptedness part.

Besides, adoption is usually a good thing because it creates a family for children who need one. Avoid regarding adoptedness as some sort of handicap. Instead, see adoption for the social good it does in our society and, when it's time to discuss adoption, explain to your child why adoption is good. (Read Chapter 11 for suggestions on explaining adoption to children of all ages.)

Your child's biological parents were not able or willing to be parents, for whatever reason. So you stepped up to the job. This doesn't mean birth parents are bad guys. Nor does it mean there was anything wrong with your child, and that's why he was adopted. (This is a common misperception among children.) But it does mean you're one of the good guys, and your child benefits by having you as a parent.

At Least Sometimes, Just Say No

Children really do need to hear "no" sometimes, no matter how hard they plead for whatever item they must have, this second. This doesn't mean you should never please your children with surprise gifts or birthday presents. But realize that children can become voracious creatures who develop a major acquisitive problem early on.

Compare the situation to a college student given several credit cards and the ability to buy whatever she wants, no limits. She may charge food, clothes, CDs, and all sorts of things on these cards, not realizing that eventually there's a payback. It'll be tough for her to face a world that doesn't react the same way as Mommy, who never says no.

Self-Test on Overindulgence

Are you an overindulgent parent? If you're not sure, take the following self-test. Simply answer each question yes or no. An analysis of your answers follows the test.

1. Your child, age eight, wants a set of drums that costs $500 for his birthday. He doesn't know how to play the drums and says he won't take lessons. He really wants the drums, and you can afford them, although you know they're overpriced. Do you buy them?

2. You made a cake for a party at school, but your child says it's yucky because it's not chocolate/cream-filled/whatever. You tell her she'll have to take the cake you've already made. You do not rush out to the fancy bakery, making yourself late to work.

3. Your twelve-year-old son asks you if he can invite a friend over. You know this child and you agree. Then another child, one whom you don't know and have never heard of before, also shows up, ready to stay overnight too. Your child begs you to let both children stay overnight. You figure it's probably okay, and let that child stay overnight too.

4. Your parents are coming over for Thanksgiving and your child, age ten, says she'd rather eat Thanksgiving dinner at her friend's house, although you're not sure why. You agree to let your child eat her holiday meal elsewhere.

5. You have more than one child and it's a gift-giving time (Christmas, Hanukkah, or some other mutual exchange of gifts). You knock yourself out trying to make sure each child receives gifts exactly the same in value.

Now, let's analyze your responses. In the first situation, if you buy your eight-year-old child an expensive set of drums for his birthday, even if you can afford them, it's usually a sign of overindulgence. It would be one thing if your child knew how to play the drums or had natural talent or was eager to take lessons. But if he just wants the drums because he wants them, it's a good thing to say no. If he pitches a fit, you still say no or simply ignore the fit. Giving in to a temper tantrum teaches a child that screaming and shouting work well, and he'll throw more tantrums in the future.

Next, in the second situation, if you made a cake for a school party and your child doesn't like it, listen to her reasons. If she has a good reason for disliking the cake, for example, her best friend is a child with diabetes and your cake is laden with sugar, you could consider making another cake or even rushing off to the bakery to get another one. But in most cases, the cake you made is fine, and your child can get over it and take that cake in. Ideally, of course, you would consult the child *before* making the cake, and even have her help you bake it.

In the third situation, when you gave permission to your child for one child whom you already knew to sleep over at your house, and another child you don't know also shows up, it would not only be overindulgent but also bad parenting if you didn't make inquiries about this other child. Do the child's parents know where he is, and did they give permission for him to come? (Call them. Don't rely on what a child tells you.) Also, if you're set up for only one extra child and don't want another child at your house, you're now in a tricky position.

You could send the extra child home, but it might hurt his feelings and put your child in an awkward position—which, as you should remember, he created for himself in the first place. Do what's best for you and your child, and don't worry about whether your little darling will be traumatized for life if you decide the right answer is to send the other child home. Your child will probably not make this mistake again.

In the fourth situation, your parents are coming over and your child is making excuses to not eat Thanksgiving dinner with them. Try to find out why. Sometimes there's a valid reason for a child's reluctance to share the big family dinner. For example, if your relatives are critical toward the child or toward you, why would your child enjoy their company? In fact, why are you putting up with their behavior?

Your family may be scandalized if you let your child off the hook for this family obligation. But if you hold her to eating dinner with the family mob and you think there may be a valid reason for her reluctance, keep your eyes and ears open. (This can be hard to do when you're in the middle of a family gathering, but do it anyway. In addition, alert your spouse or partner as well.) And if anyone actually does go on the verbal attack, tell that person politely that we don't talk that way in our family.

You can then let the child leave to go play and let off steam when dinner is over. However, once you've stood up for your child, risking the annoyance of other family members, you may find she's less eager to escape from home. Instead, she may want to stick around and see what happens next in this interesting new development. You may also find other family members were uncomfortable too and are glad you spoke up. They just didn't want to rock the boat either, and they're now glad that you did. However, keep in mind that criticism of a family member is definitely best done in private rather than in public, whenever possible.

If the reason why your child doesn't want to eat with the family (especially an adolescent) is mere boredom, it's a good lesson to learn that people (including children) have to learn to tolerate many kinds of social situations, even ones that are less fun than they'd like them to be. So she stays, eats the meal, and then can be excused.

If you have more than one child, as in the fifth situation, and you're going to great lengths to make sure that if you spent $110 on Susie's Christmas gifts, you're going to get as close to $110 as you can for Mary's gifts, this is silly. Although you shouldn't spend $110 on Susie and buy gifts totaling $10 for Mary, it's not necessary to give yourself a migraine about being totally equal. Nobody can do it, and you shouldn't even try. Most children don't know the exact price of things anyway.

Apologize When You're Wrong, Then Be Quiet

Another common error is to believe adults should never apologize to children. At the other extreme, some parents are always apologizing at great length to their children, and that isn't good either.

Contrary to what some novelists think, love *does* mean saying you're sorry sometimes. If you scream at your child, overreacting to a minor infraction because you're sick or overtired, you should apologize. Explain that you don't feel well and you're sorry. If you have been unfair, most people, including your children, will respond to your statements of regret.

Don't overexplain, because then it doesn't sound like a real apology. "I'm sorry I yelled at you, but I missed the bus and my boss yelled at me" usually isn't as well-received as "I'm sorry" or "I'm sorry. I'm having a bad day, but it's not your fault."

Nor must you rush out and buy your child something or take her for ice cream if you've made a mistake. An apology alone is sufficient and shouldn't be an opportunity to gain something material as retribution.

Boundary/Privacy Violations: Don't Let Your Child Make Too Many

Everyone deserves some privacy, including you, whether it's because you want intimate time with your significant other or you feel like being alone while you read a book. Or maybe you want to have lunch with a friend with no kids around. All parents, adoptive parents included, deserve to set some boundaries, whether it's their time, possessions, or other boundaries. Of course, babies need plenty of time and have no idea about privacy or boundaries. They eventually learn you are a different person and not just an extension of themselves. But as your child grows older, it's important to teach her to respect your privacy.

If you give your child all your time (or money, attention, and so forth) you can become resentful. You may also fail to attend to your own needs, the needs of your partner or other children, or your work.

Your possessions, including your own clothes, jewelry, and other items, should be respected as your property. If you want to allow your child to play "dress up" sometimes, that's fine. But it's not a good idea to give your children open season on whatever you own.

Overindulging a child can create an overly selfish person. The child takes whatever she wants of yours, and if she loses your stuff, she doesn't care. (Ironically, if you ever lose the prized possession of such a child, you'll certainly hear about it.)

If you find that your child is constantly taking things from your room, you've warned her to stop, and all reasonable consequences have not worked, there is one simple solution of last resort. Put a lock on your door, and turn a deaf ear to your child's cries that you're mean, you don't trust her, and so on. When boundaries have been broken, it's time to reestablish them. It's not mean or unloving. It's common sense.

Don't Fail to Acknowledge Your Child's Feelings

Another common error of well-meaning parents is to deny a child's negative feelings or try to talk the child out of them, whether they feel sad, angry, or experience another negative emotion. Of course it's normal for you to not want your child to feel upset. Yet at the same time, sometimes children will be annoyed or distraught for good reason.

Lena says she has trouble coping if her child Tiffany, age four, cries about anything. When Lena found that Tiffany's cat Spotty had died, she took Tiffany to her grandmother's house for the day. Lena then spent the entire day searching for a cat that looked just like Spotty, hoping Tiffany wouldn't notice the difference. The child *did* notice and was angry and upset with Lena for having tried to fool her. Lena realized sad things happen sometimes, even to children. She apologized to Tiffany for the deception, and said she'd never do it again. She told Tiffany Spotty had died, and they both grieved. Lena said the new cat would have a different name, since he wasn't Spotty. They decided upon Blackie, since the cat was mostly black.

Then Lena and Tiffany talked about Spotty, what a fine cat he was and how much they'd miss him. That night, Tiffany prayed Spotty would be watching her from heaven.

Don't Delay or Avoid Immunizations

Some parents have expressed strong concern over whether common immunizations can actually harm their children. They may delay the immunizations as long as possible or try to fight against having their children immunized at all. As a doctor and a parent, I think this behavior is a serious mistake.

There have been some minor problems in the past with a few lots of vaccines for immunizations, but the overwhelming percentage of vaccines are safe, and they're also quite needed. I worry about parents who try to fight their doctors over their children getting immunized. What often happens is they read a hysterical article on the Internet or in a magazine (or maybe watch a TV documentary, meant to be shocking and upset viewers in order to boost TV ratings) and start to worry their children will develop severe problems from an immunization.

If your child isn't immunized, she's not only at risk of contracting the disease but she's also at risk for spreading it to other children.

If you're worried about immunizations, talk to your pediatrician about it and express your concerns. He or she should be able to alleviate your fears.

Particular Behavioral Problems

Sometimes your child's behavior is a problem or she may need help with an eating disorder or a sleep problem. Nonadopted children may also have such problems, and it doesn't necessarily help to concentrate on whether adoption is the reason that your child's having this problem. In most cases, instead, it's important to identify ways to help the child. Sometimes therapy is needed. Read Chapter 16 for information on how to identify a possible emotional problem and what to do if one may be present.

Eating Problems and Disorders

Most eating problems that children develop are temporary or minor. However, sometimes they can become serious problems. Your common sense task is to work on sorting out the minor from the major problems. You also need to learn how to evaluate a serious eating disorder. For example, if a child insists on having ketchup with every meal, is this a minor problem or major problem? Different families react differently, and some families will say give her the ketchup, while others decide this is a control issue, we are the parents and you never have ketchup with broccoli.

Use your common sense and choose your battles wisely. Young children can have strong food preferences, and these can be very fickle. Maybe she'll want peanut butter sandwiches for lunch for weeks, and then one day she'll announce she hates them and wants something else. That's a common childhood behavior and not an eating disorder. Of course, you need to make sure your child is also eating fruits and vegetables too.

A Real Problem or Not?

If your child has some issues about eating, work on determining whether it's a serious problem, and if so, make a plan to cope with it. Also, remember that even if a child has an eating problem, it could be a temporary one. For example, if your child announces she's now a vegetarian and you're a meat-and-potatoes kind of family, is this really a disaster for you? Think about it.

When you use common sense, you'll see such behavior is rarely a major problem. In most cases, you can let your child be a vegetarian for a few days or weeks, and then she'll probably get bored with it. Or maybe she'll stick with her vegetarian eating habits for a long time. As long as she's getting enough vitamins and minerals to be healthy, she'll be fine. (Consider giving her a daily multivitamin if you're worried.) Also, think about this: since many physicians encourage most people to load up on fruits and vegetables, your child might actually be eating more healthfully than you are.

Sometimes the eating problem is a serious one. If your child is gaining or losing a lot of weight and doesn't seem to have normal control over what she eats, then she could have a problem.

Talk to your child about it. The problem could have nothing to do with food. She may be eating too much or not enough because she's sad about a problem with school or a friend. Before you rush out to get the cavalry (in the form of a nutritionist or a therapist), see if you can determine what the problem is yourself. Ask questions, in a nonthreatening way, when the child isn't upset or overtired. You may find that the problem is solvable. It's also a good idea to talk to your pediatrician or family practitioner, who can help you sort out serious problems from less serious ones.

Why Children Have Eating Problems

Why do some children have temporary eating problems, while others never do? It may be because of a change in the caregiver, even when the child is a baby. It's not only the caregiver that has changed, from someone else to you, but also the child's diet is usually different, the environment is different, the climate may be different, and many other factors may be involved. Even if you adopt a child from the United States, relocating her from San Antonio to Boston still means a different diet, climate, and so forth.

Children often need time to adjust to a new situation. Some children (and some adults) may react to such moves by eating much more or less than they did in the past or than you would consider normal for a child.

This may be especially true for children who were adopted from other countries. Maybe they were never quite sure when the next meal was coming or *if* it was coming. Such children, when adopted, may actually eat until they throw up, in a sort of irrational stockpiling tactic. Others hoard food, hiding it under their bed, in their closet, or anywhere. They need to learn they'll have enough food from now on.

In the meantime, however, they may drive their new parents crazy with their overeating and hoarding. Some parents cope with the problem by giving the child her own cupboard in the kitchen, telling her that all the food there is hers, and no one else can have it. (This may not work that well if you have more than one child.) Others continue to tell the child that food is plentiful and hope eventually the child will realize they're telling the truth.

Other children may continue with bizarre or long-term eating disorders, and may exhibit problematic behavior that must be treated. It's also true that some nonadopted children have serious eating disorders, such as anorexia nervosa (a form of self-starvation) or bulimia (bingeing on food and then making themselves throw up). Experts believe such behaviors are psychological problems that need to be treated with therapy and/or medications. Consult your pediatrician if your child is exhibiting indications of these disorders.

Sleep Problems and Disorders

Most children can readily fall asleep and are easily awakened, unless they're ill or upset. But some children experience chronic problems with insomnia, while others are difficult to wake. Some children also have serious problems with nightmares or "night terrors." These sleep problems may be related to adoption or they may not be.

Sometimes it can be difficult or impossible to determine the cause of the sleep problem, and instead you'll need to concentrate on developing a common sense approach to helping your child get a good night's sleep.

Sleep is very important for all humans, but especially for children. The production of growth hormones goes up at night. People also dream at night. But sometimes the dreams that children have can be frightening or even terrifying, and children need parents who'll help to chase away the monsters of the mind.

Should you just let the child sleep with you every night? Some experts think it's a fine idea, while others believe a child should sleep in her own bed and in her own room, after receiving comfort following a bad dream. Do what's comfortable for young children. Most people believe it's okay to occasionally let your school-age or younger child sleep in your bed. Adolescents should sleep in their own beds.

After drinks of water, reading stories, and saying prayers—or whatever bedtime rituals you use—it's time to go to sleep. (And if you don't have bedtime rituals, it's a good idea to establish some. Children are comforted with rituals and patterns.)

Sometimes children resist giving up the day and going to sleep, feeling they may miss something. This is especially true after a happy day. The child may also be overwrought or overtired, or something else may be going on in his or her life. Here are some basic dos and don'ts for helping the average child go to sleep.

Sleeping Dos	Sleeping Don'ts
A drink of water at night is okay.	Avoid more than one drink, in most cases. Too many pre-bedtime or nighttime drinks for most preschoolers will wake the child up.
Consider a small glass of milk or a piece of turkey as a bedtime snack. Milk and turkey contain tryptophan, a natural chemical that can help induce sleep.	Don't give your child chocolate or items with caffeine several hours before bed. The National Institutes of Health says caffeine stays in the system at least three hours after it's consumed.
Make sure the bed is comfortable and has a good mattress.	Don't insist all lights must be turned off if a child is fearful. Provide a night-light. Let her keep the door open if it helps.
Have dinner at least several hours before bedtime.	Don't feed your child at 8 p.m. and put her to bed at 8:30. Her body's still digesting, and it can be hard to get to sleep.
Set regular bedtimes and stick to them.	Don't let a child decide her bedtime.
Choose an age-appropriate bedtime.	Don't expect a ten-year-old to go to bed at 7 p.m. on most nights. But neither should she be up to 11 p.m. or later.

Coping with Nightmares and Night Terrors

All children have nightmares and some children have night terrors, when they wake up in a state of extreme fear and may not recognize their parents or where they are right away. In these cases, lead the child back to his bed and comfort him as best you can until he falls asleep. Keep in mind that unlike nightmares, children do not remember night terrors.

Sometimes the child has a pattern of nightmares that can be really exhausting for the sleep-deprived parents. The child really isn't trying to torture you or even test you, when the nightmares are real. (And you can usually tell when they are, by the child's overall demeanor of wide eyes, shaking body, and so forth.) Work with your child's pediatrician to try to find a solution for the problem.

Working on Frequent Wakenings

When you're the parent of an infant or toddler, you're going to face night-time wakenings. But sometimes when you adopt an older child, he may also wake up frequently at night. Work with your little insomniac. Comfort him if comfort is needed, preferably in his own bed. Get a good night-light to scare away monsters. Establish a calming bedtime ritual, and consult your pediatrician if needed.

Problems with Staying in Bed

What if you have a child who doesn't want to stay in her bed, and who keeps popping out of it? Maybe she'd rather sleep with you, or sleep anywhere else except her bed, such as the living room sofa, the family room chair, and so forth.

Generally, it's best to encourage the child to sleep in her own bed, and not in yours, because you and your spouse or partner need privacy. (Except for when a child needs occasional comforting and your child is under the age of ten or eleven years old.) But if the child wakes up and wanders off onto the sofa, not to watch TV, but maybe because she likes it there better, it's not a national disaster. As long as she's getting enough sleep—at least seven or eight hours per night—it doesn't really matter if that sleep is attained in her bed or on the sofa. However, it's a good idea to transfer the child to her own bed once she's asleep, to acclimate the child to sleeping in her bedroom. A throw pillow from the couch can be brought into the bed as a transitional object and compromise.

Part II

AS THEY GROW

6

What Bonding and Attachment Mean to You and Your Child

ALL ADOPTIVE PARENTS want to bond with their children and form a mutually strong attachment. And nearly all succeed at forming a happy and positive relationship. Yet some adoptive parents, especially newer ones, worry about bonding and attachment and whether they're doing things "right" to maximize the experience. In addition, some adoptive parents buy into the popular myth that biological parents have a magical secret connection to their children, one that usually enables them to know exactly what to do and when to do it. (Some biological parents may *think* they have such a mystical link, but there's no evidence of such a presence.)

It's natural for adoptive parents to have some doubts, especially when the media, and even family and friends, think biological parents are always better. It's important to counter those doubts with reason, which is one of the goals of this chapter and this book.

The good news is that not only do most adoptive parents have strong relationships with their children, but there are also often actions you can take to improve your relationship with your child, even if the adoption occurred years ago and your child is a teenager now.

This chapter covers the basics on bonding and attachment, including ways to evaluate your current relationship. In addition, the issues of whether some children are incapable of attaching, and the impact of "separation and loss" (a phrase often used in adoption) are addressed, as well as how to consider your sense of entitlement to your child.

Bonding Is a Process; Attachment Is the Result

Before you can analyze the relationship you have with your child and consider ways to improve it, you need to understand the basics about bonding and attachment. "Bonding" is the *process* by which a parent and child (whether an infant or an older child) become emotionally linked, whereas "attachment" describes the link that exists once bonding has occurred. Bonding is akin to applying strong glue that holds two parts together. The glue hardens, and the parts are tightly connected, or "bonded."

Attachment is the end result of the two parts being "glued" together. You can't have an attachment until you first have a bonding. And once you have a parent-child attachment, it's very difficult to break, because the emotional glue that holds you together is stronger than any epoxy ever could be.

Yet many new adoptive parents (as well as some biological parents) are confused about bonding; for example, often they don't realize bonding and attachment aren't always instantaneous. Some parents and children attach quickly and in other cases, regardless of whether the relationship is biological or adoptive, developing an attachment takes longer. You also need to understand there will be ups and downs along the way in your relationship with your child. You can't always be on the receiving end of only smiles and hugs. Sometimes parents have to be the "bad guy" disciplinarians.

In addition, attachment is not a one-way relationship, where you pour knowledge, love, and affection into your child's waiting and passive mind and heart. Instead, although you should be the adult in charge, you'll have a highly interactive relationship. Attachment is a reciprocal relationship, and a back-and-forth process between you and your child. Thus, if there's an attachment problem, it's usually not just the child's problem, nor is it necessarily your fault. Sometimes things just happen. It's also true that in some cases, older children who were adopted from orphanages or other institutions have trouble attaching to parents.

It's important to understand that you affect your child *and* your child affects you. You give love and receive smiles, responses, and yes, eventually receive love from your child. Your child is special to you and you'll become special to your child.

You hold a lot of the power and control in this relationship, as well as a lot of the responsibility. It's a two-way relationship, but definitely not a fifty-fifty even split. If you expect complete equality in the give-and-take with your child, you'll be disappointed. On the other hand, it should not be a relationship in which you give and the child only takes, which is also lopsided and potential for trouble.

Background: Bonding and Attachment

Some experts, such as psychoanalyst John Bowlby, began writing about bonding and attachment in the mid-twentieth century. Bowlby's initial research, described in his 1951 monograph for the World Health Organization, was largely based on research on institutionalized children. Bowlby deduced that if children didn't have a strong relationship with their mothers by age two and a half, the child's future life and character might be at risk. Many researchers today dispute this finding. Bowlby's research had a positive effect in that it revealed that children in institutions needed much more personal attention than they were receiving.

One bonding study still commonly cited was described by Doctors John Kennell and Marshall Klaus in the *New England Journal of Medicine* in 1972. The researchers studied twenty-eight poor women who had just given birth, dividing them into two groups. In one group, the women had much extra contact with their babies (for that time period), while in the other group, the mothers were given the babies for five minutes and then separated from them for six to twelve hours. The researchers concluded the early-contact mothers had a better long-term relationship with their babies.

The study by Klaus and Kennell had the benefit of changing hospital policies in the 1970s and beyond to allow new mothers more time with their babies. It also had the negative effect of causing women who couldn't see their babies right away, such as ill mothers or adoptive mothers, to worry they couldn't bond properly. Subsequent researchers have determined that the sample size was far too small to apply to all mothers. In addition, studies with larger sample sizes using the same methods found little or no effect on the bonding of the mothers with their babies.

Many studies indicate that children adopted as infants or young children form strong attachments to their new parents more easily than children adopted at older ages; however, some older children find it hard to attach and others don't. In fact, how well older children can attach to others is largely determined by how resilient they are.

Resiliency refers to a child's ability to function well despite past hardships the child has experienced. Most people think the more abuse a child has faced, the less resilient she'll be. But research doesn't bear that out. Some children are very resilient despite a horrible past, and can readily attach to new adoptive parents. Others will have a more difficult time making the adaptation.

Scientists know some children are more resilient than others, but are not sure why. Some experts speculate that a past positive attachment to anyone, including a parent, relative, neighbor, or friend, allows some children to withstand a difficult life. But it's difficult for social workers to predict which children who are adopted will be resilient and which won't be. There are too many unknown variables to make such predictions.

Attachment, Adopted Children, and Adoptive Parents

Many adoption studies have demonstrated that adopted children develop strong attachments to their adoptive parents as well as to their siblings and extended families. In turn, most adoptive families form strong attachments to their children.

There are some basic observable patterns about attachment and adoption. For example, in general, as mentioned earlier, the younger the child is at the time of the adoption, the more readily a new attachment is formed. As social worker Deborah D. Gray put it in her book *Attaching in Adoption* (Perspectives Press, 2002), "Children adopted as infants have been shown to enjoy higher-than-average rates of secure attachment with their parents." As a result, babies and their adoptive parents usually form strong attachments, although no one should expect instant love from day one.

This is a key reason why many people want to adopt babies. They instinctively know they will have a good chance of forming a strong mutual attachment with a child who has not known another parent for long. They also want to parent a child from early infancy and watch the child grow and mature, guiding her along the way. That's not to say that children adopted at an older age can't attach to their adoptive parents. But developing an attachment in these cases may take longer and may be a rockier road for both parent and child, depending on the child, previous attachments she has formed, and other factors.

Retaining Common Sense About Attachment

Attachments are not usually formed instantly, especially when the adopted child is not an infant. (But even infants and their biological parents don't always instantly connect.) Common sense dictates that most people, including parents and children, need time to form a lasting bond.

Even in the case when a parent has not bonded to a child, it is still possible to be a good parent. What's important is the sense of commitment to this child, no matter what.

Linda had trouble forming an attachment to Sonia, a three-year-old girl she adopted from Russia. Sonia was hyperactive and always getting into trouble. Linda was a patient woman, but she felt Sonia was destroying her home and her life, and not very slowly. Linda told herself this was a commitment she'd made, and she wouldn't give up on Sonia. And she didn't.

Gradually, Sonia began to learn about things like boundaries (that it really wasn't okay to take Linda's clothes out of her bureau and strew them about the house, or worse, outside), and she began to discover and then know Linda was her advocate. Sonia began to exhibit signs of affection like little hugs, and Linda found herself responding. The attachment blossomed. Linda knew some women might have given up on Sonia early on, but she was very glad she never considered that option.

But what if all of Linda's efforts hadn't worked? Let's say it's five years later and Sonia, now age eight, is stealing items and exhibiting other problem behaviors such as lying, skipping school, and so forth. In that case, Linda might have needed to have Sonia evaluated for an emotional disorder, as discussed in Chapter 16.

Adoptive Mothers and Attachment

Are adoptive parents just like biological parents in every way? It probably depends on what you're talking about. For example, on average, adoptive parents are better educated than the average biological parent, and they also have smaller families: many adoptive parents adopt one child or, at most, two children. But if the issue is the concern and love that parents feel, in most cases, there doesn't seem to be any difference between adoptive parents and biological parents.

In their book *Mothers and Their Adopted Children: The Bonding Process* (Tiresias Press, 1983; out of print), Dorothy W. Smith, Ed.D., and Laurie Nehls Sherwen, Ph.D., described three primary stages in which attachments form between adoptive mothers and their children.

Time 1 is a period that occurs before a child arrives in the family. In this stage, the mother fantasizes about the child and engages in activities such as preparing the child's room, buying clothes, and so on. Many adoption agency experts have noted that families "bond" to photos of children they plan to adopt. Sometimes the adoption doesn't go through, and parents undergo a grieving process, even though they never met the child.

In this stage the attachment is one-way, unless the child is an older child who has seen photos of the prospective adopters and wishes to be adopted by them.

In Time 2 the child arrives in the family, and the family and child interact. Smith and Sherwen recommended that extended family members be present at the point of first contact with the child; however, I believe it's best for the initial contact to be a private one between parents and children. They need time to interact, even when the child is an infant.

Time 3 includes the time after first contact, when the family really gets to know the child by talking to her, hugging her, and providing care. The child will respond, although sometimes not in the storybook way adopters expect. For example, children adopted from foster care or an orphanage may be very anxious about the loss of their previous home, no matter how wonderful you are or how much that child will love you in the future. They may test the parents by behaving badly to see if you'll send them away.

Considering Your Own Relationship with Your Child

If you're worried you and your child may not have a strong attachment to each other, ask yourself some basic questions. Then read the sections that discuss each issue.

1. How long has the child lived with you?
2. Is the situation better, worse, or about the same as when you first adopted your child?
3. Have there been any indicators (even minor ones) of a developing attachment?

How Long Has Your Child Lived in Your Home?

How much time the child has lived with you matters a lot. If you're worried that you and your six-year-old child don't have a strong attachment (keeping in mind attachment is a two-way interactive process), but he's only been living with you a month, give it more time. The rule of thumb is, the older the child is, the more time he needs to attach to a new parent.

This doesn't mean an older child or a teenager will take years to develop an attachment to your family, although she may. It's impossible to say how long each child might take to bond to a family. I can't tell you that for every year of age, the child needs one or two months to become attached. I can only say it usually takes longer for older children to attach to new parents.

Evaluate the Situation: Is It Better, Worse, or the Same?

When you're looking at the level of attachment between you and your child, it's important to see it from various perspectives. For example, compare the attachment level you're experiencing now to the level that was there in the first few weeks or months after you adopted your child. Is the situation better, the same, or worse?

Important caveat: if your child is on the cusp or has already plunged into the abyss of adolescence, be careful with your evaluation. You may have had a good relationship with your eleven-year-old daughter, but then she's twelve, goes through puberty, and hates you. This is usually not an attachment problem, but instead is something many parents of adolescents in all too many families are familiar with!

Considering Any (Even Slight) Indicators of Attachment

Carly was worried her two-year-old son, Jacob, whom she'd adopted several months ago, was not attached to her, at least not as much as her sister

Mary's son Bobby, also two years old, was attached to his mother. Carly wondered what she could do to improve the situation.

What Carly should do is consider the context of the situation. Bobby has never known any other parent figure since his birth but Mary. In contrast, Jacob has lived with several different people in his brief life. Even though the two boys are about the same age, Jacob's had a very different life up to now than Bobby has seen.

Considering if there were any possible examples of an existing attachment, even minor ones, a thought flashed into her mind. Carly thought about when she was in the supermarket and the checkout clerk admired Jacob, as did the bagger. The two adult women both stared at him, telling Jacob he was a very handsome boy. He burst into tears and hid his face with his hands. Carly hugged Jacob, and he buried his face in her shirt, wrapping his arms around her as tightly as he could. In turn, Carly hugged Jacob and told him everything was going to be all right. Carly and Jacob had a strong attachment.

And yet, at first Carly didn't realize that Jacob's behavior was actually a good thing. She wondered if Jacob was too shy or maybe she wasn't that good of a parent. But she thought about it more and realized Jacob was afraid of strangers, which meant he didn't like them staring at him. This is a normal stage of development. Carly realized Jacob was attached to her because he responded to her and wanted and needed her reassurances.

In his groundbreaking book on attachment, John Bowlby essentially described such a situation as Carly's supermarket one, in very formal language. Here's what Bowlby (who was British) said in his book *Attachment and Loss* (Basic Books, 1980):

> The systems mediating attachment behaviour are activated only by certain conditions, for example, strangeness, fatigue, anything frightening, and [the] unavailability or unresponsiveness of [the] attachment figure, and are terminated only by certain other conditions, for example, a familiar environment and the ready availability or responsiveness of an attachment figure. When attachment behaviour is strongly aroused, however, termination may require touching, or clinging, or the actively reassuring behaviour of the attachment figure.

Thus, Jacob was frightened by the behavior of the strangers in the supermarket and the unfamiliar attention. (Even though the people in the market were being friendly.) When his mother responded to his fear by comforting him, he responded by clinging to her and then calming down. Clearly, Jacob and Carly have a mutual attachment, just as Bowlby described it.

Attachment Doesn't Mean a Perfectly Harmonious Relationship at All Times

It's also important to know that having an attachment between you and your child doesn't mean you'll always be happy with your child or vice versa. Sometimes you may become angry or annoyed with him, and sometimes your child will think you're the worst parent in the world. But the basic underpinnings of the attachment are there, like a concrete foundation of a house. If you didn't love your child, you wouldn't care about his behavior, and, in turn, he wouldn't much care what you thought of his behavior either.

How Attachment Varies by Age

The type and intensity of attachment varies with many factors, and one of them is the child's age. As mentioned, if you adopt an infant or small child, generally the attachment will be formed more easily than when you adopt an older child. This is because older kids have had many experiences before you adopted them. Don't assume that they come to you as a blank slate. They don't.

If you're adopting an older child, he may have been abused or neglected. (Or both.) He may need to learn to trust that an adult isn't always someone who's mean and who hurts him or leaves him.

Attachment Among Babies and Toddlers

Babies and toddlers indicate their attachment to you by smiles, holding out their arms to you, and by preferring you to others. Sometimes these responses take a while in coming, when you adopt an older child or a child from an orphanage. In other cases, parents worry because their child is indiscriminately friendly to just about everyone.

However, in a 2002 study, reported in the *Journal of the American Academy of Child and Adolescent Psychiatry*, the researchers found that indiscriminately friendly behavior among children adopted from Romania occurred among children who were securely attached to their parents as *well as* among children who hadn't developed an attachment. The researchers concluded that indiscriminate friendliness may be an issue that's separate from a lack of attachment to adoptive parents.

The researchers studied sixty-one children adopted from Romanian orphanages, evaluating the children at eleven months after the adoption and then thirty-nine months after the adoption. They found that a majority of the children were indiscriminately friendly to others. But they also found the security of the parent-child attachment significantly increased over time, although indiscriminate friendliness to strangers didn't change among the children adopted at eight months or older.

Said the researchers, "We found clear evidence that indiscriminate behavior may be observed in children with and without an attachment figure. This result is in keeping with findings from follow-up studies of children adopted out of institutions indicating that indiscriminate behavior persists even after children have formed attachments to their adoptive parents."

Of course, if your child runs to every stranger, this is a problem you'll need to deal with. However, the point is you shouldn't see such behavior as an automatic rejection of you or an indication that your child isn't attached to you. This should reassure many parents.

Former Attachments Children May Have Made

Most children form strong attachments as young children to their primary caregivers, usually their parents. Even children who are abused or neglected may still have attachments to their parents. Thus, it should not be surprising that children adopted from foster care may still love and grieve for their biological parents, despite abuse and neglect at the hands of their birth parents.

It's hard for many people to understand how or why a child could love an abusive parent, but the reality is that they can and they do. Attempting to talk a child *out* of loving an abusive parent is an exercise in futility, so don't try it. Instead, read how to explain abusive behavior to your child (and to yourself) in Chapter 11.

Attachment Among Older Children and Teenagers

Attachment between you and an older child or teenager you adopt can take plenty of effort, but will usually happen. Older children have had life experiences that may have been very negative and difficult, and they'll almost inevitably test you to see if you can put up with their behavior. They may curse, have tantrums, or exhibit a wide array of negative behaviors. Will you send them back? Will you react in some other way? They're watching you to find out.

Considering Yourself in Relation to Your Child

Because a parent-child relationship is highly interactive, it's important to consider issues affecting both you and your child. For example, it's a good idea to consider your feelings of entitlement to your child, and whether you feel you're worthy to be a parent. It's also important to consider differences in temperaments and personalities and work to resolve conflicts that arise because of these differences.

Your Own Feelings of Doubt

How do you know if you doubt your entitlement to be your child's parent or if you are doubting your parenting skills? Ask yourself the following questions by answering yes or no. Keep in mind all parents feel inept at some point, so answer in terms of how you feel most of the time.

1. I assume that my sister or friend always or usually would be a better parent than I am.
2. I wonder if my child's birth mother or someone else in the birth family would "know better" what my child needs.
3. The home study process made me wonder and worry about whether I could handle parenting.
4. I know I'm doing my best and I'm willing to learn more to help my child.

With questions 1 and 2, if most of the time you feel other people, including the child's birth family, could do a better job than you, you may be experiencing a problem of insecurity. If you feel unworthy or incapable, you could make some serious parenting mistakes, such as failing to correct your child when discipline is needed or overspending on gifts to compensate for perceived inadequacies. You can't replace the birth mother, but you can be a good parent in your own right. You need to find your own "voice" as a parent.

The fact is, the social worker (or God, if you're a religious person) approved you to adopt this child, and it's up to you to step up to this task. Square your shoulders and get on with it. If that doesn't work, identify a counselor who can help you challenge your personal qualms about your parenting skills. And work on improving those skills.

The home study process can be daunting, as mentioned in question 3. It's meant to screen people who really want to make a commitment to a child from those with a passing fancy or who are incapable of parenting because of problems with alcohol or drug abuse or other issues. It's also meant to raise questions in your mind about how you plan on parenting your child. These are good issues to consider. But if your home study made you feel inadequate, you may have entitlement problems that carry over in your relationship with your child. It's also possible you had a perfectionistic or insensitive social worker who made you feel unworthy. The home study is over: the child is home and needs you to be a parent. Don't worry about what a social worker said or did. Instead, do the right thing for you and your child now.

If you answered yes to question 4, you most likely don't have a problem with doubts. No one's perfect, and if you're doing your best and things are generally going okay, then this is the way life is.

Temperamental Matters

Parents and children are often very different, whether children are born to parents or adopted by them. You may have a very aggressive and athletic mind-set, whereas your child may be a drifty and dreamy bookworm. Or the situation may be the other way around. If the child were born to you, you might think she was "just like" your Aunt Alice or some obscure relative. If your child was adopted, you can't say who she's like. But does it really matter? After all, the birth child might not really be like Aunt Alice at all, and it's merely a perception. The point is to acknowledge the child's temperament, accept it, and work with her.

One advantage of adopting a child is that you usually don't expect the child to be your temperamental clone. Whether you're calm and carefree or a hyperactive worrier, you (hopefully) don't assume the child will be just like you. Understanding that temperament matters, you realize that what motivates you or stresses you out may be very different from what motivates or disturbs your child, and you adapt to those needs.

Truly "Unattached" Children and Families: Do They Exist?

Some people seem to believe that many or most adopted children have severe problems with attachment or can't attach to anyone. Or they may think most children adopted from other countries can't attach to a family, or that children who fit other situations (such as children of a different race than their adoptive parents) can't attach to new families.

Sometimes people who have experienced serious problems with their own adopted children find great comfort in generalizing their sad situation to others, whether it is truly relevant to others or not. They think because their experience was very negative, everyone who adopts a child from the same country (or from foster care, or from a situation that fits the experience they went through) will inevitably be miserable, just like them. Misery not only loves company, it sometimes actively seeks it out. Yet your experience may be very different from theirs.

However, some children really do have difficulties with attaching to new parents, and this is especially true if they are school-age children or older or are children who have been severely abused or neglected in the past. The differences in attachment among school-age children who are adopted hinge considerably on their preadoption experiences.

Putting "Separation and Loss" into Perspective

Many social workers and some authors worry a great deal about separation and loss in relation to adoption. Some people think children can never recover from not being reared by their biological parents.

There are also others who seem to believe everything will be just wonderful if adoption issues are ignored—although few people will publicly state such a viewpoint.

Separation and loss are issues that adopted children face, and how they deal with them depends on a variety of factors. A common sense approach involves considering some key issues, including the following:

- Taking into account the age of the child at the time of the separation from the birth parents or other caregivers
- Considering the age of the child when adopted (since not all children are adopted right away)
- Factoring in the child's temperament and personality (some children are anxious worriers, while others are more easygoing)
- Taking into account major life changes that occurred in the child's past (such as moves, births, deaths, major illnesses, and experiences of abuse or neglect)

The Child's Age When Separated from Primary Caregivers

The age of the child when separated from a biological relative or other person with whom the child has developed a relationship is significant, even if the attachment occurred as an infant. Most experts believe if a child has been able to attach to an adult, even if the attachment wasn't problem-free, he'll be able to form an attachment to another adult. As the old maxim goes, "Better to have loved and lost, than never to have loved at all."

In most cases, the younger the child is when you adopt him, the more likely he'll form an attachment with you. The problem may come with children ages three and over, particularly children who've been living in orphanages with many caretakers and no one person who really cared about the child. The child could have lived in a nice, clean orphanage and been given sufficient food and medical care. But if she was treated more like an object than a person, this child may have trouble bonding with adults later on. She just has no frame of reference.

Some experts believe attachment is like a milestone that must be met by a certain age, and if it hasn't been met, it can't ever be met. Others actively disagree.

Considering Major Life Changes, Such as Moves

Some children are adopted as infants when they are days old. Others are removed from their families because of abuse or neglect and may not be adopted for months or years. In addition, some children are moved from one foster family to another foster family, and may live with ten or more families. If the child "acts out" with bad behavior, she is more likely to be "bounced" to another foster family. If you adopt this child, how does she know *you* are a keeper? She doesn't, and you can expect that you'll be tested.

Past Abusive or Neglectful Experiences

If your child has been abused or neglected in the past, it can take time before he can learn to trust you as someone who doesn't hit or hurt, as well as someone who pays attention and provides food and clothes. The child may try to goad you into losing your temper, to test what will happen if you do. This may actually be a positive sign (although it doesn't seem like one!) because the child cares enough to try to find out if *you* care enough.

Strengthening the Bonding Glue

Regardless of the age of your child and even when you adopted him or her, there are nearly always actions you can take to improve your relationship. Here are a few ideas to consider, which you should tailor to the age of the child.

- Work on a project together to create something, whether it's a garden that you plant together and regularly water and weed or something more elaborate.
- Go places together as a family. Go on picnics, to movies, and on vacations. Before you go, ask your child what activities she would like to do, and if possible, do them.
- Share the hard times. Although you shouldn't ask your child what to do about difficult adult problems, when you're ill or out of sorts, tell your child if things are hard right now. Allow your child to help you,

whether it's making a simple breakfast, getting you a cup of water, or just hugging you. (Or all of the above!)

Key Bonding Concepts

Decades of research on bonding and attachment have produced some key observations:

- Children and parents usually form strong attachments with each other.
- Attachments can often be observed in the behavior of the child and the parent.
- If children don't form attachments in early life, it can be harder (or in rare cases, impossible) for them to attach to others.
- Strong attachments in early life enable children to form other attachments to people later, such as parents, friends, spouses, and others.
- Adoptive parents can and do love their children as much as biological parents. Love doesn't require a genetic link.

7

Raising Your Infant and Young Child

PARENTING YOUR BABY, toddler, or preschool child can be fun, exhausting, maddening, and hilarious—often in the same day—and you'll experience many other emotions as you help your child navigate her way toward big-kid-ness.

This chapter addresses parenting issues related to your baby and young child, including dealing with your family and others on advice they offer you, coping with your fears, and handling children's behaviors. Breastfeeding is also briefly discussed, because some adoptive mothers wish to breastfeed their babies. Keep in mind this should be *your* choice, not imposed by others. Another topic addressed is potty training, usually done sometime after a child is two years old, depending on a child's individual readiness and ability. The rest of the chapter is devoted to issues related to basic discipline for young children.

Dealing with Family, Friends, and Others

As soon as you become a parent, whether your newly arrived child is a newborn, toddler, or older, you're launched on a path with a multitude of parenting choices and decisions that must be made. Nor are you operating in a vacuum. If you're married or in a relationship with a live-in partner, he or she will also be affected by and affect this small person. If you have other children, they'll interact with the child. Even extended family members like grandparents or uncles, as well as unrelated people like neighbors and friends, will weigh in with advice. This can be good or bad, depending on the person, the situation, the child, and the advice.

Expect Lots of Unsolicited Advice

You'll probably never receive as much parenting advice in your life as you'll hear about what you must do (or *not* do) until your child is about five years old. Complete strangers will tell you to bundle up your child better because it's cold outside. Or they will watch how you react in the supermarket if your three-year-old throws a hissy fit because she's overtired or sick. If others don't approve of your child's behavior (or yours), you'll hear about it. Of course, if your child is quiet, strangers may comment on "good" behavior too. However most people notice screaming children more readily than quiet children.

Most people think it's perfectly okay to offer unsolicited commentary to any parent. Be open to outside advice, but selective about which advice to follow, using common sense. Remember, even strangers can be helpful. They may point out when your child is doing something dangerous, giving you a heads-up chance to react in time.

Other times, people offer annoying remarks. In most cases, it's best to ignore them rather than argue, especially if they're strangers whose behavior you can't predict.

When It's Advice for Adopters

Because all new parents receive advice from others, don't assume it's because you've *adopted* a child that other people are telling you how to do everything. Most people have no idea you adopted your child. For example, if you are Caucasian and your child is African-American, you could be married to a black person, for all strangers know. There's no sign over your head that signals "adoptive parent" to others, nor is there a similar sign over your child's head indicating "adopted child."

However, sometimes adoptive parents receive unsolicited advice from people who *do* know you've adopted. Sometimes the advice makes sense, and other times it's nonsensical. Your task is to sort it out so that you can make the best choices for your child.

In most cases, parenting advice you receive from family members and friends is well-meant, even if it may seem silly. No, your grandmother isn't lapsing into senility because she's worried your cat will smother your baby while he's asleep. It's a superstition, and you probably won't be able to talk her out of it. Thank her and assure her you'll keep a close watch on kitty.

Others may advise you on how to bond with your child better, particularly if you're having trouble bonding to a newly adopted child. Check with your pediatrician if a therapist or anyone else recommends you institute any parenting practices that sound questionable to you.

As explained in Chapter 6, bonding is a process by which you and your child become close to each other, and attachment is the cemented relationship between you. The attachment between you and your child is uniquely defined by who you are and who your child is, in temperament, energy levels, and many other ways.

Don't Worry Too Much About Lags in Growth and Development

Many parents are eager for their children to achieve various milestones of childhood development, but most pediatricians agree there's considerable variability among children as to when they first talk, walk, and achieve other aspects of growing up. If you adopted your young child from another country or from foster care, cut her some slack. She may need extra time to achieve developmental milestones. However, most experts agree children adopted as babies and toddlers can achieve remarkable "catch-up."

For example, in 1998, Dr. Michael Rutter and his colleagues reported in the *Journal of Child Psychology and Psychiatry and Allied Disciplines* on 111 children adopted from Romania before the age of two years by their new parents in England. When the children were first adopted, more than half (51 percent) were below the third percentile in weight, which means 97 percent of other children that age weighed more than them. When the children were reevaluated at the age of four years, only 2 percent were at this low weight.

This doesn't mean all children grow normally after they're adopted. What it does mean is that a positive and caring environment can help children achieve more than what they're capable of in a negative environment.

Sometimes you may worry your child lags behind in growth or development, not just a few months, but much more. Talk to your pediatrician about this. Many pediatricians know that U.S. growth charts may not be useful in the early stages after you've adopted, before your child has a chance to catch up to other children. As a rule of thumb, many children lose about one month of growth and development for every three or four months spent in an institution. However, a 50 percent delay in growth or development is a matter of greater concern. For example, if a child was adopted from an orphanage at the age of one year, and he's at about the nine-month developmental level, that's reassuring. But if the same child is at or below the six-month level in growth or development, this is troubling.

Keeping that information in mind, your doctor may recommend you consider an early intervention (EI) program or special education preschool for your young child. These programs screen children for difficulties with language and motor skills and provide treatment services when appropriate. These programs may trigger needed development to the next stage. They are free to the child, and federally and state funded. They are also beneficial for children with developmental disorders, such as mental retardation, autism, cerebral palsy, and other medical problems.

It's not magic, but some early intervention programs can help children considerably. (Find out about such programs from your pediatrician, your local school board, or the state education or health department, usually located in the state capital.)

Coping with Fears: Everyone Has Them

Parenthood can be difficult sometimes. What if you do something wrong? What if you *don't* do something you should have done? These fears are normal parenting anxieties. You may also worry that you should be there for your child, as close to 24/7 as you can manage. However, I recommend regular brief breaks for parents and children from each other. Getting together again is refreshingly wonderful.

Being Good Enough

Some parents worry about whether they're good enough parents, and if they "deserve" to be parents—even though they *are* parents now. I discuss feelings of entitlement to your child in Chapter 6. People who feel they're good enough for their child are happier in their relationship with their children.

If you worry about measuring up, tell yourself you'll do the best you can, although you can't be a perfect parent. If you still struggle with feelings of doubt about your entitlement to your child, talk to adoptive parents about it in a local adoptive parent support group. (See the Appendix.) In many cases, your family and friends can also provide good support to you.

Sometimes feelings of inferiority loom very large, and may mean you have a problem with depression or anxiety or other issues that need to be dealt with. In such a case, it's wise to talk to a therapist who can help you sort out your feelings and concerns.

Some therapists use cognitive-behavioral therapy (CBT), a form of therapy that helps people identify irrational and unreasonable thoughts, such as "I'm a terrible mom because I yelled at Carly! She'll be traumatized for life!" People learn to replace such irrational thoughts with others, such as "I wish I hadn't yelled at Carly, but I did. I need to count to ten when I get annoyed. For now, I'll go apologize to Carly."

In some cases, parents need antidepressants or antianxiety medications, if their emotions are overwhelming and therapy alone isn't enough. It doesn't mean you're bad or crazy if you need medications. In most cases, it would be worse to not take them if your negative emotions kept you from functioning adequately as a parent.

Taking Regular Breaks

Be sure to get regular time off for yourself. Ask your friends, parents, or other trusted people to babysit so you can go shopping alone or to lunch with friends. It can be overwhelming to be with a child day in, day out, whether your child was adopted or not.

If you work, as many parents do, you may feel you're already away from the child so much, it's not fair for you to take extra time off beyond work time. Work is time away from your child, but for most people, it's not "down" time from stress or responsibilities in the same way that engaging in activities you love is. Schedule time off without your child at regular intervals. Be sure to schedule time off with your significant other too. Couples need time alone together on a regular basis, even if it's taking a walk together without the kids. (Avoid talking exclusively about the children during time together.)

Making Mistakes

You'll make parenting mistakes. Everyone does. You may forget to buy diapers or take longer than you think you should to get up to comfort a young child with a bad dream. As long as you avoid abusing, neglecting, or abandoning your child, most mistakes are correctable and forgivable.

Sometimes small children injure themselves as they charge around the house or outside. Doctors are aware of normal patterns of injuries, and can nearly always tell the difference between an injury caused in the course of a child who's playing versus an injury that was incurred as a form of abusive punishment by parents or others.

Thinking About Breastfeeding Your Baby

Some adoptive mothers choose to breastfeed their babies, but don't let anyone tell you you're a bad mother if you decide not to breastfeed. Also, please avoid feeling morally superior over other adoptive mothers if you *do* opt for breastfeeding. Adoptive mothers who choose to breastfeed use a supplemental nursing system that enables the baby to suck on the breast while also being fed with formula. Some mothers use breast pumps and/or take medications to stimulate actual lactation; however, supplemental formula is virtually always needed by the baby.

With breastfeeding, you attain virtually the same closeness that biologically breastfeeding mothers achieve. However, nonbreastfeeding mothers can also hold their babies close and cuddle them.

Contact La Leche League International (lalecheleague.org) for information on breastfeeding an adopted infant. You may also wish to check other resources on the Internet, such as the Adoptive Breastfeeding Resource website, available at fourfriends.com/abrw.

Potty Training

In years long past, parents were expected to toilet train children by the age of two years old at the latest. If your child wasn't trained by then, you were considered a bad parent. Now the rules have eased up, and most parents want their children toilet trained by the age of three. Most children are capable of being trained by that age, but some children take longer to achieve this milestone.

If your child was adopted as an infant and has developed normally so far, you probably won't have great difficulty helping your child with potty training, although it's still work and takes time (months, not weeks!) before your child achieves bladder and bowel control. If you adopted your child as an older child, age three and older, and the child isn't trained, don't make potty training your number one priority upon the child's arrival. You may need to use big-kid diapers for a while until your child adjusts. In most cases, and fairly quickly, children will notice the toilet and be interested in using it and you'll have the chance to provide that training.

Some men are willing to show little boys how to urinate into a toilet. Women usually don't sit on a toilet and urinate into it to show a girl how to urinate, although they may. One caveat however: don't expect little boys to have the careful aim of their fathers and hit the toilet water dead-on. There will be some misses outside the toilet. Tell your son to try to hit inside the toilet. (You can also make a colored mark on the toilet paper and put it in the toilet, and offer that as a targeting challenge to your son.)

For numerous excellent hints on helping your child to achieve toilet training, I recommend *Potty Training for Dummies* by Diane Stafford and Jennifer Shoquist, M.D., a book that covers routine situations as well as a variety of difficult problems that may arise, such as with disabled children or children who are very reluctant to use the toilet.

Some signs of readiness for potty training are if your child has fairly regular bowel movements and sometimes notices in advance that he has to go. If the child is dry at least two hours at a time, this is another indicator of possible readiness. Another indicator is if your child doesn't like the smell or feel of a dirty diaper or is able to tell you that he's wet or dirty.

Expect some nighttime accidents two or three times a week after toilet training has "taken." Most nighttime incidents end when a child is around four or five; however, about 10 percent of children still wet the bed after that age, mostly boys. Continue reassurance and talk to your pediatrician about it. Be sure to tell the doctor if your child complains of burning with urination. Even small children can develop bladder infections.

Catching Your Child Being "Good"

Rewards and punishments are an important part of raising your child. But keep in mind that often your child's behavior is not planned. Few children decide to misbehave, although they may fall into aggravating behavior patterns that involve whining, begging, and so forth.

One effective way of helping children to improve their behavior is to catch them in the act of being good. This requires patience as well as vigilance. Most parents ignore good behavior and complain about bad behavior, when the fact is that praising good behavior is very effective.

Here's an example. Nora adopted two brothers, Timmy, age five, and Jimmy, age three, from foster care. They constantly bicker about everything. But one day, Nora notices that Timmy and Jimmy are playing quietly and happily together. She doesn't know how long this will last, and her first inclination is to just leave the boys alone. But then she decides that she'll praise Timmy and Jimmy for their good behavior.

Nora gives them both a big beaming smile and tells them she is so happy that they're playing nicely. And, because they're behaving so well, they can go to the park in a few minutes if they'd like to. Since Nora knows the boys love feeding the ducks at the park, she also knows that it's a reward they'll jump at accepting. As they drive to the park, Nora again praises Timmy and Jimmy for getting along together so well. Nora realizes that her sons will argue again, maybe even this afternoon or sooner. But she's working on cutting back the frequency of arguments by noticing when they *don't* happen.

Here's another example. Cindy adopted Nadia and Sonia, ages four and five, from Russia last year. They are generally very well-behaved, but for some reason, every time Cindy gets on the phone, Nadia and Sonia really start acting up until Cindy is forced to end her phone conversation. Nothing Cindy has tried to improve this situation has worked.

One day, the phone rings and it's her sister. Ten minutes into the conversation, Cindy notices that Nadia and Sonia are not clamoring for attention but are individually playing with their dolls. Cindy ends the conversation and praises the girls lavishly for being quiet while Mommy's on the phone and hugs them. Nadia and Sonia seem surprised but very pleased. The next time the phone rings, Nadia starts to act up, but Sonia shushes her, telling her stop it, Mommy's on the phone!

In fairly short order, good behavior has become routine. Cindy still needs to give praise for good behavior, but often a smile and a hug is all the girls need to reinforce their quietness when Cindy's on the phone. On her end, Cindy keeps the conversations reasonably brief because she knows little girls get impatient with very long phone calls.

Coping with Common Behaviors of Small Children

Even toddlers learn quickly when they can control their parents, whether it's smiles or screams that work best. By the time they're young children, they can be masterful at getting what they want. This is not to say your child is some sort of Svengali at the age of three, practicing for her future as the ruler of the world. It's normal behavior.

Young children quickly discover what behaviors achieve the responses they want. If your two-year-old finds out the first request for a cookie gets a no, but if she screams loud and long enough, a no eventually transforms into a yes, she'll learn to scream for her cookies.

This is not a good pattern for you to set. Consider the analogy of a slot machine. If sticking coins in a machine hardly ever pays off, but once in a while pays off big-time, some people will be drawn to slot machines. Thus, if screaming behavior gets you to do what the child wants even sometimes, she learns it's an effective tactic.

It's also important to realize young children believe if Mommy can't see something, she'll believe it's not there. If you think Tiffany has pilfered some cookies, you can ask Tiffany, who has both hands behind her back, to show you her hands, and then, when she does, tell her that you see that she does have the cookies, and take them away from her.

This behavior is very normal for a small child. Don't give little Tiffany an extended lecture about the importance of telling the truth. She won't understand what you're talking about—not until she's much older.

It's Okay to Say No to Your Child

A lot of parents have trouble saying no to their children. They may reason that they waited so long to adopt, or the child suffered in an abusive home in the past and deserves to have it easy now. Or they may worry they are not good parents unless they mostly (or nearly always) say yes to their child.

They may also be enchanted by the cute little child, reasoning they can easily afford whatever the item is the child wants. Even if they know a child doesn't need it and will forget it in ten minutes if the item is purchased, they still buy the thing. In my case (Dr. Adesman), my own priorities with parenting are in this order: safety, health, and then the happiness of the child. If it's not safe, my answer is no. If it's unhealthy, it's again no. In addition to physically dangerous or unhealthy experiences that I veto for my children, when I deny my children some items or experiences, it's because it is detrimental to their emotional or mental health, such as indulging them with excessive treats or inappropriate liberties; for example, I won't allow my ten-year-old child to see movies that are rated PG-13 or R.

There's a place for limits, either as a function of a child's age, to maintain parity with siblings, or to defer gratification until it's earned.

All parents need to say no in the interests of their children, whether they were adopted or not. It helps to foster character, self-worth (and not self-entitlement), and the child's place in the family, and it also helps children appreciate what they have. The rest of the world will have no trouble saying no to them, and it's best if they hear it first at home, where they know they're loved for themselves.

Basic Disciplinary Issues for Toddlers and Small Children

Most small children have only a rudimentary understanding of what's considered good and bad behavior. They won't always act in the way you wish, but neither are they bad children because they don't behave exactly as you hope.

Keep It Simple

The best way to discipline small children is to make very simple rules that are easy to understand and to follow. It's also important for a child to understand when the rules are broken (and they will be, even if only to test you meant them), so it's best to react quickly and consistently, so the child will learn that misbehavior relates to a consequence.

Avoid giving your small child a detailed explanation of why she should do one action, but avoid doing another action. Just tell the child what the rules are. Later, when your child is a school-age or adolescent person, your rules will be regularly challenged, and you may have to justify them then. But not when your child is little. Maybe you swore in the past you'd never say, "Because I said so," just like your own parent. However, this is actually an okay thing to say to a small child.

Be Consistent

If you tell Timmy he must go to bed by 8 p.m., and some days you enforce the bedtime and others you don't (for no reason), this is frustrating for your child. Children like to know what's expected. Sure, they like surprises and fun things. But household routines about eating and bedtimes and other basic rules should be followed. Not rigidly, but on a regular basis.

Be consistent in your punishment. If you discipline a child for an infraction and then the child does the same thing later and you don't react, this is confusing to the child. Does the behavior matter or not? What is it Mommy wants? It may be that on one day you're feeling sick or too tired to follow the rules you've set up, and that's okay. In general, however, stick to the disciplinary and behavioral patterns that you've established with your child.

As your child gets older, she'll argue for exceptions to rules or routines, and it's reasonable to consider these requests. Some examples are for an extra cookie (for no reason) or an extra story at bedtime. On the other hand, parents need to develop a manner in which they clearly indicate when there's no further room for discussion. When my children were in preschool, I signaled the subject was closed by saying, "Absolutely not," or, "No way, no how." My children knew it was pointless to try to change my mind then.

Tailor Discipline to Your Child

Some small children, ages three to five, may respond to simple punishments, such as "time-outs," when a child is separated from activities as a consequence and, for example, stands in the corner. Time-outs are best done in a supervised but nonstimulating setting, such as the corner of a hall or the bottom stair of a staircase.

The consequences that you set should take into consideration the following parameters:

1. Does the child understand the behavior is unacceptable?
2. Can the child behave in the manner that you wish?
3. Does the punishment fit the "crime"?
4. Can the consequence occur shortly after the unfortunate behavior?

Can the Child Behave in the Manner That You Wish?

Make sure the behavior you're seeking is something your child is capable of performing. If you're expecting your four-year-old son to never wet his bed, is that a reasonable expectation? Many pediatricians would say no, because bedwetting is common among small children.

Shaming your son or yelling at him will not solve the problem if it's a physical one or a problem of delayed maturity. Talk to your pediatrician about what to do to help your child if he has this problem. Another common unrealistic expectation is to expect a young child to remain well-behaved as she's dragged along for an entire day of shopping at the mall. That would be equivalent to expecting you to be fresh and alert for over twelve hours, and just as unrealistic an expectation.

Tailoring the Punishment

The severity of the punishment should depend on what was done, as well as the age of the child who did it. If the child spilled something, an accidental act should usually not be punished, although you may wish to have your child help you clean it up so he can see the consequences of his acts.

Even if the child gets into major trouble, such as purposefully breaking something valuable to you or purposely using colorful language while talking to his shocked grandma, there's only so much punishment you can hand down. Keep in mind a ten-minute time-out is usually too long for a three-year-old but is reasonable for a fifth grader. A rule of thumb for time-outs is one minute for each year of age. One good behavior management book I recommend is *1-2-3 Magic: Effective Discipline for Children 2–12* by Thomas Phelan, Ph.D.

Can the Consequence Occur Shortly After the Unfortunate Behavior?

Sometimes problem behavior can't be corrected right away. Try to avoid the "Wait until your father/mother gets home" mentality, if you can't discipline your child soon after the behavior occurred. The child may imagine all sorts of dreadful things happening until then, and may see his other parent as the "bad guy." Also, if the situation occurred between you and the child, you should mete out the punishment. If you can't do so, tell the child why you're upset, for example, because he broke Aunt Sarah's vase while running around her house after you told him to sit down.

It's also possible to establish time-outs when you're away from home. When my children were younger, I told them in advance where the time-out corner was in the supermarket. I also reminded them of my expectations while we were there. Keep in mind that although punishments should be as immediate as possible, it's important to keep your own emotions in check when meting out punishment.

Often parents can achieve a lot by mastering simple behavioral techniques such as consistency, establishing effective motivators tailored to your child's age and interests, and anticipating possible problems. It's also important to consider whether your rewards for good behavior are effective. For example, if reward stickers lose their novelty or value as a motivator or positive reinforcement, then speak with your child so that you can mutually identify other more desired rewards.

Considering "Normal" and "Abnormal" Behavior: How Do You Tell the Difference?

You may wonder if behavior exhibited by a child is in the normal range or if it's abnormal behavior that requires therapy. This is a brief section because Chapter 16 addresses how to determine if your child needs therapy and how to find a good therapist if one is needed.

To determine if your small child's behavior may be outside the normal range, ask yourself the following questions, and read the section devoted to each question.

1. Is the behavior harmful to the child or to others?
2. Is the behavior repetitive or something the child did once?
3. Is the behavior annoying but typical for small children?

Harmful Behavior

If your child is constantly banging his head into the crib, the wall, or another object, this is generally not normal behavior, although head-banging is certainly seen in some formerly institutionalized children who are adopted. Maybe the child has an ear infection or severe headache, or is exhibiting distress over another problem. Ask your pediatrician to evaluate the child for a physical problem.

Let's say little Jacob, age three, is hitting other children in his play group. Children do hit other children, and it isn't abnormal. But if your child is aggressively going after other children, this may be problematic behavior. Try to see what's bothering Jacob. Are you expecting him to share his toys, and he doesn't understand the concept of sharing yet? Talk to your doctor about it. (And supervise Jacob closely when he's with other children until the hitting problem is resolved.)

Frequency of the Behavior

You may become concerned if your child exhibits strange behavior. For example, if a child occasionally pulls on her hair, this is generally normal behavior. If the child constantly pulls on her hair, and has pulled out a lot of it, this is an indicator of a problem that you should ask your doctor about.

Annoying But Typical Behaviors

Small children can perform irritating (to adults) acts, such as picking their noses, making fart noises on purpose, and other behaviors. Of course you should curb unsanitary behavior, but don't overreact. Tell the child in a matter-of-fact manner that fingers don't go in noses. As for the fart noises, you may be stuck with those for a while, although you can teach your child to forgo making them in your presence or in public by giving a consequence if he performs them.

Joyous Parenting Experiences

Through the daily concerns and difficulties over dealing with behavioral issues, the fact remains that raising a baby or young child brings many joyous and wonderful experiences, such as the first time your child recognizes you as Mommy or Daddy and prefers you to all other people who want to hold her. Or the first time your child achieves a major milestone, such as taking that tentative step that leads toward walking. Sharing your preschooler's joy at a new pet can also be a wonderful experience, as can the pride you take in your child mastering toilet training and other major milestones.

8

The School-Age Child:
Ages Five to Twelve

As YOUR CHILD grows into a school-age child (or perhaps you adopted your child after she had begun school), new parenting challenges and opportunities will present themselves. This chapter addresses key issues, including how to help your child deal with others who are confused about adoption and may ask embarrassing or intrusive questions. It also covers how to cope with some of the aggravating comments your child may make to you, such as telling you her "real mother" would be much nicer than you are.

Adopted children have an added burden to what's experienced by other school-age children, in that sometimes people say disturbing or offensive statements to them, including comments that are purposely mean and others that are based on ignorance.

Sometimes teachers can be a problem, such as teachers who assume adopted children can't achieve as much or as well as nonadopted children. Or teachers (and sometimes even parents!) may have unreasonably high expectations.

Many parents agonize over whether they should tell their child's teacher the child was adopted. Also, if you tell a kindergarten teacher, should you later on tell the first grade teacher, second grade teacher, and so on? (Just because information is in a child's school record doesn't mean teachers will read it. They have many students and little extra time.)

In addition, some school activities can be distressing to an adopted child. The family tree exercise is a school exercise that has distressed adopted children for years, but which (hopefully) is assigned less frequently now, since there are many "blended" families of children with divorced parents, stepparents, never-married parents, and other parental configurations. Such children would also find the exercise confusing and upsetting. This chapter offers suggestions on how to handle the family tree exercise.

Grades are a very big issue for many parents. If your child is getting mostly Cs and you'd really prefer that she were an A or mostly an A and B student, are your expectations for these grades truly reasonable? Expectations were discussed in Chapter 4, but it's worth briefly revisiting the issue here.

Another aspect of the school-age child (age five through twelve years old) is that your child's friends will usually become very important and you'll sometimes find yourself in a second-place role to that of your child's best friend or even to any friends. This is normal and a part of growing up. But it's still important, of course, to keep track of who your child's friends are and what activities they're involved in, and this is another issue covered in this chapter.

Confusing Things Said to Adopted Children

Plenty of confusing things are said to adopted children, sometimes even by family members, but more frequently by people outside the family. Some of these comments may come in the form of questions, while others are statements. Here are a few examples, with discussion of ways to help your child respond to them.

Who's Your Real Mom and Why Did She "Give You Away"?

No matter how hard adoptive parents try to teach others, including their children, about positive adoption language, it's inevitable sometimes they'll hear messages about adoption that are couched in negative language. The most classic example is the question, "Why did your real mother give you away?" The wording of the question alone sets the teeth of most adoptive parents on edge.

There are actually two hurtful parts here, including the "real mother" and the imagery of "giving away" the child, a seemingly callous act. And yet children can't be given away like puppies or kittens. Only a court can legally end the parental rights of the birth parents and transfer them to the adoptive parents. Or, to put it more simply, only a judge can say an adoption is legal and permanent. It's against the law for parents to sell or give away their children.

It's best if you discuss with your child possible answers to this intrusive question. Some children tell others their "real parents" are their adoptive parents, but that often doesn't solve the problem, even though it makes their parents happy, because the questions usually persist. Tell your children many people are nosey about what's going on (or went on) in other people's lives, and this is just one example of such nosiness. Your child may choose to answer the question, if she wishes to, or can tell the person she doesn't wish to talk about it, also a valid answer.

If the child wishes to provide an answer to the "real parent" issue, one good answer, also discussed in Chapter 11, is that the birth parents were unable to be parents and that's why she was adopted. Of course, this begs the question of *why* the birth parents were unable to be parents, and the child may not wish to go further than this point. If she does, she may wish to say the parents were too young or were from another country where they couldn't parent more children, or some other answer.

Some people press children surprisingly hard for more details, and at some point the child needs to stop the conversation, when it exceeds her comfort level. This can be done by simply asking, "Why do you want to know this?" including saying it repeatedly, if necessary. The child can also say, "I don't want to talk about this anymore," closing the subject. Be sure to tell your child she has the right to not answer questions from others, including other adults and even teachers. As a parent, give your child permission for privacy, so it can be used like a free pass, when your child has a need for it.

You can have practice conversations with your child in which you play the role of Obnoxious Person (or you speak the lines for a doll or a toy) and your child provides answers back. Ham it up as much as possible to take some of the sting out of the subject and to help your child reframe the issue in her mind.

Have You Met Your "Real" Mother Yet?

Because so many adoption "reunion" shows have been depicted on television between adopted adults and birth parents, many people have assumed that all adopted children and adults will eventually wish to meet their birth parents. The reality is that some adoptees seek such a meeting while others don't, and both are normal responses. No one knows how many adopted adults meet their birth parents, but it's probably less than a majority of cases. However, when it comes to adopted children under age eighteen, they usually don't interact with a birth parent unless the adoption is an open one.

The question of "have you met your 'real' mother yet" is very intrusive (and the phrase "real mother" offends most adoptive parents), because it implies most people do meet, and if you haven't or don't want to, then you're weird, which is the last thing most kids want to be.

Remind your child some people are incredibly nosey, and he doesn't have to answer such a question other than with the words "No," "Not yet," or "I don't want to talk about that."

Some adoptive parents have also fallen into the trap of assuming all adopted children wish to meet their biological parents, and have pressed their children to go ahead and work on arranging such a meeting, with their help. My position is very simple on this issue. It's up to adopted adults if they wish to meet their birth parents, and no one else should make that choice for them. They should also decide when the time is right; it's not your decision. You can offer help and support, but leave the choice to the adopted adult.

I Always Thought I Was Adopted

Some people think it's interesting or even humorous to tell adopted children they always secretly believed that they or someone else in their family was adopted, because they (or the other person) didn't resemble other family members or were different in some other way. Imagining that maybe you were adopted but knowing you really weren't is not the same thing at all as actually being an adopted person. To respond to such a silly comment from another person, your child could give a brush-off comment such as, "Oh really, how nice," said in a polite but flat voice.

What's It Like to Be Adopted?

One question that's very hard for most adopted children to respond to is how it feels to be adopted. In many cases, the child has no basis for comparison because she was adopted as an infant or small child. Being adopted is the only experience she has to draw memories from, because she has no recall of *not* being adopted.

A similar question is if children are asked how they *like* being adopted or how they like this family they're in. For most children, it's not a question of liking or disliking their family, but rather it's just the way things are. It may be comparable to asking a person from the United States, who's never left the country, how she likes being an American. Or asking a Caucasian how happy she is being white, and how she likes belonging to this ethnic group. What else is there, for that person?

To such questions, a simple answer from your child such as "I don't know" or "It's okay" or a similar comment, with a change of the subject, is usually the best response.

Confusing Things Your Child May Say to You

Because of confusing and conflicting feelings that may arise as your child grows, sometimes he may say things that can distress you. Here are some key examples of adoption-specific comments, with basic advice on how to cope with each one.

My Real Mother Wouldn't Make Me Do That

Some parents say their children have never said, in anger, that their real parents wouldn't make them pick up their clothes, do chores, be home by eleven, and so forth. And maybe your child will never say it to you either. But if he does, take a deep breath and don't defend yourself as a good parent, compared to the birth parent or anyone else. Instead, it's usually best to say you are the "real" parent, and your rules are to do so and so. You may also wish to add that nearly all parents have rules and you aren't unique in that respect. And if your child had never been adopted, he'd be following someone else's rules.

A variation on "my real parent wouldn't make me do that" is "You're not my real parent and you can't make me do that." Calmly tell the child you *are* the parent and he must follow your rules. Count to ten in your mind so you don't blow up. Then assume the child will follow your rules. If he doesn't, impose an appropriate consequence.

I Wish I Wasn't Adopted

Some children tell their parents they wish they'd never been adopted. This could be a reflection of the sadness they may be feeling about being adopted—or could be sadness about how adopted children are sometimes depicted in our society as losers and emotional cripples. You know if your child had never been adopted, he wouldn't be your child, and that hurts. Wishing he wasn't adopted may sound like a rejection of you as a parent, although it usually isn't meant that way.

Tell your child you're wondering if he's sad about his birth parents. Listen to what he has to say. Then be sure to tell your child you're very glad you adopted him, although you appreciate sometimes it can make him sad.

Sometimes your child may tell you he wishes he had been born to you, which is a very positive statement to make, showing his love for you. You may wish to respond by saying you also wish he'd been born to you, because you love him so much. You could also say that you couldn't possibly love your child any more than you do.

Dealing with Peer Groups

As your child grows, having friends becomes increasingly important. Occasionally, you may find yourself in the position of having to prevent your son or daughter from socializing with a child you consider undesirable because of the other child's behavior. This will usually antagonize your child, but keep in mind it's not your job to be your child's best friend. Instead, you're the parent. And sometimes that's your child's least favorite person, because you're considering his safety and health first, and then his happiness.

It's upsetting when your child is very angry at you, but you need to keep him or her away from other children who are engaging in illegal or questionable activities or whose behavior seems out of control to you.

When Your Child's Grades Are Cs—and She's Really Doing Her Best

If your heart is set on having a student who receives all As and Bs, but your child brings home Cs (or maybe even a few worse grades), this can be disturbing. Is C work good enough? It is if it's the best your child can do.

If you aren't really sure what your child's capabilities are, you may wish to have your child's intelligence tested. If your child has an average intelligence and is obtaining average grades, she's performing within her capabilities. To expect higher grades would be unreasonable.

It's also possible your child is a bright person with a learning disability, and to determine if one is present she'll need psychological and educational testing. Sometimes parents must press school officials hard to obtain an evaluation through their school district at public expense. Some parents hire psychologists privately to perform the evaluation. If a problem is found, they're then armed with ammunition to present to school district personnel. If these individuals don't listen, parents may wish to consult with a developmental pediatrician or an educational advocate to help determine what is reasonable and appropriate.

Discipline and the School-Age Child

Babies and small children don't understand the difference between right and wrong, but as your school-age child grows, she should develop a conscience and basic sense of what is good or bad behavior. Of course, corrections will sometimes be required by you, the parent.

Time-outs are effective punishments for school-age children (ages 5 to 12 years) when used properly. Being made to stare at a blank wall is a benign but effective form of negative reinforcement or punishment. With time-outs, the rule of thumb is to add one minute for each year of the child's age.

You may wish to use other punishments. As an example, if your ten-year-old child uses obscene language in your presence, you can "ground" him from watching television for the evening or from going out with his friends. You should also tell him outright that you disapprove of such behavior. It's also best if you, your partner, and any other family members also avoid using the same language that got your child into trouble.

Working with Teachers

Talking about adoption with others is discussed in Chapter 12, including whether or not to tell teachers your child was adopted. More details on working with teachers are provided here.

The Pros and Cons of Telling Teachers Your Child Was Adopted

An advantage of telling teachers about your child's adoption is that they may be more understanding about academic or social problems your child is experiencing. In addition, in some cases, parents choose to help teachers prepare a unit on adoption to educate the other children. (It often helps to educate the teachers too.)

The key negative of telling your child's teacher about adoption is that the child is more likely to be viewed as pathetic or a person who has problems or is bound to have them in the near future. This may be very far from the truth for your child, and if teachers start treating him differently, he'll notice it and won't like it.

Dealing with Problematic Teachers

Sometimes you may encounter teachers who are not understanding of your child, and sometimes the problem isn't the child, it's the teacher. She may have racist ideas, assuming your Chinese daughter obviously must be good in math and science since she's Asian, and clearly (to the teacher) isn't trying hard enough since she's failing math.

In most cases, a simple parent-teacher meeting can resolve misunderstandings or confusion that a teacher has about your child, whether the issue has to do with adoption or not. As mentioned, maybe your child has a learning disability that needs to be evaluated. Or maybe your child needs to be seated closer to the front of the classroom to avoid paying more attention to her friends than the teacher.

Sometimes, no matter how hard parents try, a teacher presents a difficult obstacle to a child's education and even to her happiness. However, there's also a tendency to believe people in authority, such as teachers, are often right.

If you're not really sure who's primarily the problem, your child or the teacher, despite discussing it with your child, then meet with the teacher and listen very carefully to what she has to say. Ask for evidence for the claims she makes; for example, if she says your son didn't do any assignments for the past two weeks, ask what the assignments were. If she can't provide that information or even a general approximation, this indicates a problem.

When your best efforts at dealing with a teacher prove fruitless and you realize she's probably (or is certainly) part of the problem, you may wish to ask for a meeting with the principal. Politely and rationally explain your concerns, and don't lose your temper. You may wish to leave the child at home, since your emotions could be inflamed if he were present. Tell the principal you'd like him or her to investigate the situation and address the problem. One solution may be to have your child assigned to another class.

In many cases, your wishes will be heeded; however, if the principal refuses your request, consult with an independent professional, such as a developmental pediatrician or educational advocate, before deciding what to do. Most parents should be able to work things out with their schools, so don't make a decision to pull your child out of school on an impulse and in the heat of the moment. But do act for the best interests of your child.

The School Family Tree Exercise

As mentioned at the beginning of this chapter, some teachers require children to draw a family tree as a school exercise, and adopted children may be uncertain about where to put their adoptive parents and their birth parents on the tree. Or should they include only their adoptive parents? Or only their birth parents? It can be quite a conundrum.

In an experience that still rings true today, described in a 1985 book entitled *The Adoption Experience* by Steven Nickman (a psychiatrist), Mr. Wall, a teacher, had chided a child for failing to prepare a family tree and for writing a frivolous family history that depicted his father as a hit man for the Mafia and his mother as a Japanese prostitute.

The teacher, obviously very annoyed, asked the child in front of all of his classmates if he actually thought that he had been properly respectful of his true origins with his story. The child responded very bravely, saying that yes, he thought that it was respectful, considering the circumstances. Then the child said, "But respect has nothing to do with it . . . Did you ever hear of adoption, Mr. Wall? Did you ever hear of not knowing where you come from, Mr. Wall? How much fun do you think that is? I think I did pretty well with your little assignment."

According to author Nickman, the shocked teacher then stared down at his desk, his white face now ashen gray, and he said, "I didn't know." And then, "You should all know something about me. Now that Jason has put the matter so strongly, with such imagination, when all I've done is avoid it." The implication was that the teacher subsequently told the class that he too had been adopted.

Of course, many teachers have *not* been adopted, nor are they adoptive parents or birth parents. The most they may know about adoption is whatever they've learned in school or seen on the movie-of-the-week on television.

If your child is given a family tree assignment, discuss with her how to handle it. She may wish to include information that will show she was adopted or may not want to share that information with the teacher and other children. Let her make that choice.

You may wish to broach with the teacher the subject of whether the family tree will be part of the curriculum at the beginning of the school year. If it will be, you may suggest it be more of a private assignment rather than a public one that's read aloud to the class. You could also approach it by helping your child realize that *everyone's* heritage comes from multiple sources. A classmate may have a father of German and Irish ancestry and a mother of African descent. Your child may be influenced by the impact of your Italian background and your spouse's Australian heritage, as well as by her birth parents' Romanian ancestry.

Coping with Common Complaints

Common complaints used by school-age children to get what they want are fairly well known, and you probably used at least some of them when you were a child too. Here are several of the most commonly used excuses among school-age children. Exploration of each one separately follows the list.

- Everyone does it or has it/no one does it or has to do it.
- If you loved me, you would let me do it.
- You treat me like a baby.

Everyone Else Does It

Whatever the desired action or behavior is, the "everyone else does it" excuse is very common, even if it may seem highly original to your child. Don't immediately count it out because you think it is a lame excuse. Are you being reasonable? After all, if everyone *is* wearing jeans and you're making your daughter wear a dress to a party, is that really fair? It probably isn't. However, in most cases the "everybody else is doing it" excuse is invalid. One way to find out is to ask your child for the names of "everybody," which you'll write down. When she asks you why you're doing this, tell her you want to check with these children's mothers, just to make sure they've all agreed to let their children do whatever the desired action is. Don't be surprised if your child is horrified and tells you to forget about it.

Social acceptance and peer-referenced norms are important to children, but they also need to be mindful (and sometimes reminded) of their own individuality. And you need to stick to rules that are important to you, even if other parents have different ideas.

If You Loved Me, You'd Let Me Do It

This statement works surprisingly well on some parents. Don't make this mistake. You do love your child, and that's why sometimes you must say no to her. She won't like it, and that's too bad. You don't have to allow the child to do whatever she wants to prove your love. She knows that you love her already. So act like a parent, and do the right thing.

You Treat Me Like a Baby

It's very common for school-age children to moan that their parents are treating them like infants. Occasionally, your child may be right that you are giving him or her restrictions that are more appropriate to a younger child. Contact other parents with children the same age to discuss the types of restrictions they give their children. Keep in mind, however, that even if every other parent allows their children to do something that you disapprove of, you should continue to stick to your own convictions.

Joyous Experiences

This chapter has centered on problems that you may experience with your school-age child. But there are many joyous experiences as well! They include seeing your child in the school play and trying not to cry with your overwhelming pride, and also trying not to jump up and down like an idiot and embarrass your child. School-age children can be delightful, maddening, and fun, as you reexperience joys from your own childhood with them as well as brand-new exciting moments together.

9

The Adolescent

IF YOU THOUGHT parenting was challenging before adolescence, most parents need to watch out! Parenting an adolescent can be a rocky road, with some smooth patches along the way. For many parents, raising a teenager is the most challenging aspect of parenthood. Teenagers frequently test your limits to their behavior, and they may think (and will often tell you this) that their parents are quite stupid and annoying.

When it comes to adopted teenagers, they may also say hurtful things, such as that they're really glad they don't have your genes and consequently can't grow up to be just like you. Take it with a grain of salt and a sense of humor, because most adolescents really do value their parents, underneath it all. And treasure those times when your teenager gives you an unsolicited hug or beaming smile.

One of the parenting challenges is to avoid being a doormat kind of parent and, at the same time, to refrain from responding in kind to your adolescent with your own hurtful remarks. If you think this could never happen to you, think again! You may sometimes feel like you're emotionally pressed up against a wall, and you have to push back to breathe normally.

Of course, parenting a teenager isn't all bad. Most of the time, it's not that hard to figure out when adolescents are testing you (or they may be testing themselves), because the behavior is out of whack with how they normally act. For example, if your teenager dresses like a preppie one day, then suddenly dons all-black clothing, and then days later is wearing the latest hip-hop fashions, she's reflecting her inner confusion.

Growing up into adulthood can be a pretty scary process. At school, teenagers criticize their peers for nearly everything. If a teen isn't "too fat," then she's too thin, or her complexion is too broken out. Or he wears glasses or she has skinny legs. Sometimes, being adopted can seem to other teenagers like another thing to pick someone apart about.

This chapter addresses common parenting problems that parents of adolescents may face, as well as challenges that adoptive parenting sometimes brings, such as coping with adolescent fears related to adoption. (Explaining adoption to your adolescent is covered in Chapter 11.)

Fortunately, several studies, such as the study performed by the Search Institute in Minnesota on nearly nine hundred adolescents adopted as babies or toddlers, have shown that many adopted adolescents are functioning well. This study, whose results were released in 1994, compared adolescents to their nonadopted siblings and found little difference between the two groups. Of course, this doesn't mean you should expect adolescence to be a problem-free period or think it won't challenge your parenting skills and your patience. Because often, it will.

Adolescence can be hard on everyone! It's also a time of self-exploration and discovery and in many ways may be a sort of "prequel" to what becomes important to your child as an adult. (Although sometimes the adult man or woman is very different from the teenage self.) In addition, once they make it through adolescence, most young adults (adopted or not) have an improved relationship with their parents.

Identity Issues

A key issue that adolescents must wrestle with is the difficult question, "Who am I?" The personal struggle can be further blurred for an adopted adolescent, who may wonder if he'd be a very different person if he'd been parented by his biological parents or by other adoptive parents than you.

Your child may directly express concerns about his identity issues to you, but more likely he'll express inner distress by sulking, ignoring you, and even offering up an occasional spate of aggressive verbal abuse—which may leave you feeling like an accused person in a surrealistic play, someone who doesn't have a clue about what crime she's charged with.

Just because it's tough to be an adolescent doesn't mean you need to play a passive role. You don't deserve to be abused verbally, and should make that clear to your child. If telling her so doesn't make an impression, use whatever consequences work with your child. Perhaps she'll respond to having her phone or computer time curtailed. It's also not written anywhere that you must drive a child to her friend's house just after she screamed at you. Actions do have consequences, which is an important lesson to learn.

Low self-esteem may be a problem for some adolescents. Study results are mixed with regard to whether adopted adolescents have lower self-esteem than nonadopted adolescents. One confounding factor that may explain the discrepancy is that some researchers include children in their study who were adopted at older ages, such as older than three or four years. Children who were abused or neglected, even in early childhood, have much to overcome.

Helping Your Child Break Loose and Also Maintain Contact

Learning how to be an adult can be a difficult task for many adolescents. Most teens make mistakes, and some mistakes are worse than others. If you think the worst thing in the world that could happen is that your adolescent daughter just dyed her hair blue *and* she's come home with a ring through her nose, many other parents would laugh uproariously at you and tell you about far worse problems they've experienced with their adolescents. This doesn't mean the blue hair or nose ring should be ignored. It's okay to express your disapproval (or amusement) to your child.

They've Got to Have Friends, but Limits Are Also Important

Sometimes teenagers (and younger children) can become involved with undesirable people who encourage them to engage in bad behaviors, such as drinking, smoking, or even engaging in criminal acts.

It's true it can be hard to control adolescents, because they're in school all day and then they're often off with their friends. And in most cases, simply disliking a friend of your teenager isn't sufficient reason to quash the friendship. But if there are specific and strong reasons why you don't like a particular person that your teenager is associating with, then explain your reasons to your teenager and say that this person isn't allowed in your house and that he shouldn't see the person outside your house either.

You also hold the financial purse strings, so don't hesitate to use that power when needed as a consequence for breaking your rules, including if your teenager continues to see individuals that you've told him not to see. You should provide food, basic clothing, and shelter. But you don't have to provide many extras desired by adolescents, ranging from makeup to expensive shoes or other items, which can be withheld as consequences to breaking the rules you have laid down.

Before slamming on the financial brakes, think about it. Make sure you're not overreacting to some harmless extremes of dress and appearance that your child or his friend is exhibiting or to merely annoying, rather than potentially harmful, behavior.

You don't have to (and should not) acquiesce to problem behaviors like smoking or drinking, and should help your child if you notice such behaviors, as well as any evidence of eating disorders, lethargic behavior, or other signs something's not quite right. Talk to your child's doctor about the problem. You may also need to consult with a counselor. At the same time, realize that no one is on an even keel at all times.

Smoking: Discourage It!

There's no evidence that adopted teens are more likely to smoke than non-adopted adolescents. However, smoking is a behavior that often starts in adolescence, so your teenager is at risk. Many studies have shown most adult smokers started smoking when they were just teenagers, and generally, this behavior began because they wanted to impress their friends. Smoking quickly became a habit very hard to break.

Smoking can lead to many health problems, including bronchitis, lung cancer, throat cancer, heart disease, and other health problems. Some problems can start at an early age, such as severe and chronic coughing from smoking. Smoking can also impede your child's performance in competitive sports, which may be important to him or her.

If your child has already started smoking, urge him to quit immediately and contact your pediatrician for help in involving your child in a smoking cessation program. Your child may need to use a nicotine patch or a prescribed medication, such as Zyban (bupropion).

Don't use any nonsmoking remedies (over-the-counter or prescribed drugs) unless you first discuss them with your child's pediatrician. Medications may not be appropriate for your child. Also, if your doctor thinks nicotine replacement therapy is in order, make sure you and the doctor impress on your child that he should not smoke *and* use the patch (or gum or whatever form the nicotine replacement therapy comes in) because some people have overdosed on nicotine that way.

Drinking: Your Child Should Avoid It

Adolescents should stay away from alcohol. It's not that adopted teens are especially likely to become alcoholics, but rather that one drunken incident could destroy your child's life, as well as others' lives.

All states set the legal drinking age at twenty-one years, so it's obvious it's illegal for a person under age twenty-one to drink. In addition, all states have "zero tolerance" laws for minor drivers, who can be charged with a crime if they have very low levels of alcohol in their system. It's *not* okay for a parent to decide a child can drink alcohol as long as he or she is at home or at a party with friends whom the parents know. (One of those friends could be your child!) Giving alcohol to your child at home is illegal and irresponsible, and it's also illegal and irresponsible for other adults to give your child alcohol in their homes. The argument that people in Europe drink before age twenty-one does not fly in the United States, which does not have that cultural tradition.

Teenage alcohol consumption leads to car crashes, unplanned pregnancies, violent behavior, and many other severe and sometimes irreversible consequences. Some kids engage in binge drinking, and others have actually died from alcohol poisoning, a condition that occurs when a person consumes too much alcohol very rapidly, so that the liver cannot metabolize it fast enough and the person's body shuts down altogether.

Sex and Your Teenager

There's no evidence that adopted teenagers are more sexually active than nonadopted adolescents; however, many teens are sexually active, and that alone is good reason to talk to your teenager about sex.

Many parents would prefer that their adolescents avoid serious sexual experiences (such as intercourse) until they're adults. And if you strongly believe in abstinence for teenagers, tell your child about your belief. Don't assume teenagers know what you expect—tell them. At the same time, parents should leave an opening so that teens who have already had sex can feel that they can still talk to their parents.

Some adolescents forgo sexual experimentation, but others will not. Especially in this time of Internet pornography and sexual innuendoes on television, in the movies, and in magazines, your child can't ignore sex, nor do the raging hormones of adolescence make it any easier. Social pressure from others can make it more difficult. ("You're *still* a virgin?")

It's best to tell your child it's important to respect a sexual partner, and that you'd prefer he or she not regard sex casually. Be sure to talk to your teenager about contraception and the importance of avoiding pregnancy until she is ready to have a child. Some people think talking about contraception will make adolescents think you're giving them tacit permission to have premarital sex, but I disagree.

Tell your teenager that it's not unmanly or unwomanly to say no to sex, and that sex should never be used as a form of thank-you for a date. Tell your teenager that oral sex *is* sex, and that it is not a risk-free behavior. Unprotected oral sex can give a person a sexually transmitted disease like herpes.

It's also good to tell your adolescent that anyone who says she should "prove" her love for him by having sex with him should be told that he can prove his love for her by respecting her wish to wait for sex until she feels ready.

Helping Adolescents Cope with Others

Adolescence is when your child will probably receive the greatest amount of negative feedback from other people his own age. If he has something different about himself, such as being adopted, he'll be teased about it— which is why many teenagers do not want to talk about being adopted with their peers.

When the most important thing in your life is to be the same as the other kids, it's tough to be different from others your own age. Some adults still agonize over their high school years when they're in their thirties and forties or even older! So imagine how difficult it may be for your adolescent, living through it right now.

One hint: when your child complains to you about others, try to refrain from saying unkind things about them, because they're likely to become his new best friends tomorrow. Teenagers can be very mercurial. Your son will remember you didn't like Bobby, although he may forget you said Bobby was awful specifically because he teased your son. As a result, sympathize, but comment on the behavior rather than the person: "Bobby shouldn't have said that! That wasn't a nice thing to say at all," and so forth.

Some Basic Coping Guidelines

You can be supportive and helpful of your adolescent. Follow these guidelines, as a starter.

1. Tell your child you're there for her if she wants to talk about anything at all. If she seems hurt or sad, acknowledge it, but don't press her if she insists she doesn't want to talk to you right now. Maybe she'll wish to talk later. (If you see signs of any apparent depression or a serious emotional problem, do press her further, and also contact your family doctor. Read Chapter 16 for further information on emotional problems.) Your teenager may be upset about something to do with adoption, but it could also be her complexion, a passing remark someone made to her that she's puzzling about, or many other possibilities.

2. If your child complains of a teacher or another adult who's being unfair, don't assume that your child must be wrong (or right). Ask for details. If your child clams up and won't provide any further details (which often happens), some parents obtain more information by using an exaggeration tactic. For example, if a teen says that Mrs. Jones is mean and gives too much homework, and then won't offer any further information, you could say in a joking tone, "I've heard that Mrs. Jones gives six hours of homework a night! I couldn't take that!" Of course, you're just making this up, which your child will quickly figure out, but she may be so curious about what you've said that she may start talking about the problem. "Mom, Mrs. Jones doesn't give six hours! It's three hours, and it's still too much," your child might say, giving you a chance to continue the dialogue.

3. Use humor when possible to lighten up the mood. It doesn't always work, but it can help when you're in the midst of a child's adolescent doldrums. You could ask your child if this bad mood was caused by seeing masses of alligators on the interstate or if he's worried about a blizzard coming (in July). Exaggeration and downright silliness sometimes help to break the ice.

4. Realize sometimes there's nothing that you can do to make your child happy, when she's in a mood and/or you're not willing to give in to an unreasonable request. Unless you fear your adolescent may be experiencing a problem with depression, don't fixate on it. Often, a few hours later, you'll hear your teenager laughing uproariously at someone's jokes over the telephone, seemingly unaffected by whatever bothered her earlier.

5. In general, adolescent boys are easier to talk to when you're working with them on a project, such as weeding the garden, painting the kitchen, or driving an hour somewhere together. Eating out in a non–fast food restaurant offers opportunities to engage in conversational bonding and sometimes may provide an opportunity to talk about serious topics. For example, simply seeing couples together could lead to a discussion of dating. Participating in volunteer activities together could also be enjoyable for a parent and a child and help improve your relationship. When boys don't feel like they're the focus of your attention as you talk to them, they have an easier time with communication. Conversely, girls are more likely to wish to be the center of your direct attention. However, all kids are different, so if the direct approach doesn't work well with your daughter, try the indirect one.

Considering Adoption Issues

By the time your child is an adolescent, she should know she was adopted and be aware of the basics behind her adoption story. You may think she never wants to talk about adoption because she's already fully informed about this subject. But teenagers can still be curious and wonder what the real deal with adoption is.

If you think your adolescent may be curious about adoption, there are plenty of opportunities to bring the subject up. For example, if you hear about a teen pregnancy program in the high school, you may mention that some teens choose adoption instead of parenting, although most don't, and see what your child says.

When you see a program on TV about infertility, you can mention to your teenager that adopting a child is a good solution for some families but it's not the right answer for others—which should pique your child's curiosity to ask you why it isn't a good solution for everyone. The answer is that some people think that they'd only be happy with a biological child, so it's a good thing that they don't adopt, because imagine how unhappy that child would be.

Don't bring up adoption around your child's friends, however, because practically everything embarrasses adolescents. If your son or daughter brings up the subject, it's okay for you to talk about it too. But try to avoid the ooey-gooey stories about how absolutely precious your son looked the first time you saw him. He'd rather hear such comments in private. And don't drag out the baby or small-child photos, because that would really mortify your child.

Adolescent Fears About Adoption

Adolescents don't think in lockstep, and they are all unique people. But some adopted adolescents may have several fears that relate to adoption. For example, they may fear they'll act out in the same way as their biological parents, including having a child at a young age or exhibiting other problem behavior. They may fear that being adopted is a stigmatizing thing and hesitate to talk about it to other people. They may secretly wonder if their adoptive parents will still love them even though they're behaving obnoxiously. (They may know they're acting up, but sometimes can't seem to stop.) They may also wonder about and even fear meeting their birth parents, if the adoption was not an open one.

Fear of Turning into the Birth Parent

Most adoptive parents tell their children about the circumstances of their adoption, and some may also share negative information, such as that the birth mother was an alcoholic or that the birth father had raped the birth mother. As children grow into adolescence, sometimes they may fear that they will become just like their birth parents in terms of their negative aspects.

For example, the girl whose birth mother had a baby (your child) at age seventeen may be afraid that she too will become pregnant when she's a teenager. The boy who knows his birth father was a rapist may wonder if he has inherited violent tendencies that he may be unable to control as he grows older. Children may fear that they may develop addictions to drugs or alcohol, just like their biological parents had an addiction. They may also fear that they may develop a mental illness like the birth parent had.

Whether your child expresses these fears to you or not, it's important to state at least once or twice during your child's adolescence that biology is not destiny, and although sometimes people inherit a predisposition to having a problem with drugs or alcohol, or a mental illness, they are not doomed to develop such a problem. Nor is it forewritten that because a girl's birth mother had a crisis pregnancy, she too must relive this experience. It can be very relieving to adolescents to hear you make such a statement.

You may also wish to emphasize your point by using people in your family, if the situation fits. For example, Aunt Tessie had a bad drinking problem, but her three adult children are fine. You might speculate that Uncle Frank's positive influence may have played a key role in that, although you can't be sure.

Sometimes adolescents may worry about what they *don't* know about their birth parents, and may exaggerate their own personal and medical flaws. Perhaps you have little or no information about the birth parents, so you can't tell your child she's wrong. But point out that in all families, some people have problems and others don't, and scientists have been puzzling over the heredity/environment issue for years, and will continue to do so.

Fear of Telling Others About Being Adopted

Many adopted adolescents are fearful or embarrassed to tell others they were adopted, especially others their own age. This fear is a valid one, because often peers will tease them about being adopted or bombard them with questions about their adoption and their birth parents. Tell your child he can decide whom to tell about his adoption, as well as what to tell. This will help empower him.

Fear of Losing Parents' Love Over Obnoxious Behavior

Sometimes adopted adolescents may fear you'll stop loving them if their behavior becomes too horrible, such as screaming at you, using profanity, breaking things you treasure, and so forth. This fear is more likely to be present among children adopted at older ages, rather than among children adopted as infants or toddlers.

Although it's important for you to set rules and punishments for when the rules are broken, it's also important for your teenager to know that your love is unconditional. You still love the person, even when you really dislike his behavior. Tell your child this.

Fears About Meeting Birth Parents

If the adoption wasn't an open one, the adopted adolescent will often fantasize about her birth parents, although she may also fear what will happen in the future. For example, if they meet, what if the birth parents don't like her? Or what if she doesn't like them? The teenager may also worry the birth parents could be dead.

If your child has expressed interest in searching for his birth parents in the future, you should remind your teenager that most birth parents are average people. They're not geniuses or idiots and they're not usually glamorous or hideously ugly. Be sure to tell your child that sometimes birth parents refuse to meet with an adopted child, but this is not the norm as far as anyone can determine. As for the fear that the birth parents have died, if you know how old they were when your child was adopted, provide that information to your child. For example, if the birth mother was twenty when you adopted your baby, and he's fifteen, she's thirty-five years old. It's unlikely she has died, although it's possible.

Joyous Experiences

Many people think about the tough times that they have with their teens and commiserate with other parents on how they ever survived adolescence. But there are also happy times that you should cherish with your teenager, even if they may be less frequent than during your child's preschool and school-age years. For example, family trips can still be fun, if you take into account your child's particular interests. You may be able to bring your child's friend along with you on the trip, making the experience more positive for both your child and you.

Realize that adolescence is a time of discovery and when your child is an adult, you and he will laugh about the misadventures and enjoy recalling the good times you had together.

10

Sibling Considerations

Siblings are important to children, whether their brothers and sisters are born to their family or adopted by them. The Sibling Interaction and Behavior Study (SIBS), a large study led by principal investigator Matt McGue, Ph.D., at the University of Minnesota, has found in preliminary results that adopted adolescents have as warm a relationship with their siblings and no greater conflicts than nonadopted children.

This chapter addresses issues related to siblings when one or more were adopted. In addition, if you're thinking about adopting another child, it presents issues to consider before you adopt.

Sibling Rivalry

Siblings often disagree with each other, sometimes heatedly. When it happens, it doesn't mean you're a bad parent. Nor does it mean the children are unstable or it's impossible for them to get along (although rarely, this may happen). Once you accept that conflict will sometimes occur between siblings no matter what you say or do, it's a lot less distressing when it happens.

Siblings clash for different reasons. They may jockey for more of your time, money, and attention. Every child wants to be the most important one to a parent, while at the same time, most parents wish to love their children equally. But when there's more than one child in the family, sometimes one child receives more attention than another. And at some points, a parent feels more or less happy with one child than another, whether it's because Child A won an award or because Child B received yet another speeding ticket.

The keys are for your children to know they're loved unconditionally and to avoid labeling any child as the "bad one" or the "good child." (Even when it may seem to work out that way.) Common sense parenting also means you give your children limits and there are consequences when they violate the rules.

In many families, birth order matters, whether children were adopted or not. In most cases, the oldest child receives the most privileges and greatest responsibilities, while younger children are more likely to get away with things their annoyed older siblings recall they could "never" have done at the same age. (Often they're right about this.)

Another factor to keep in mind is a preliminary finding of the SIBS study researchers. In a 2003 interview Matt McGue, Ph.D., the principal investigator, said that younger siblings are significantly influenced by older children, particularly when older children engage in problem behaviors such as smoking, drinking, and disobeying their parents. This is true whether younger siblings have a genetic relationship to an older child or not.

The SIBS study, funded by the National Institutes of Health, was launched in 1998 and will continue through about 2008. In this study there are 966 children, including 586 adopted children. All the children were adopted as infants or toddlers under the age of two years old, and about two-thirds were adopted from other countries than the United States. Most of the children were under age one when they were adopted.

As of this writing in 2003, the average age of the children is fifteen years old. Most of the adoptive families include parents who adopted one child and then later adopted another child, although some families adopted a child first and later had a biological child. Very few families had biological children first and then adopted a child.

So far, the preliminary findings of the study track many previous studies, which have shown that children adopted as infants or toddlers generally have no greater risk for mental health problems than nonadopted children.

When You Have a Biological Child Either Before or After Adopting

For most families comprised of adopted and nonadopted children, the issue of adoption doesn't matter to the children involved any more than the entry of a new child through birth would trouble them. This doesn't mean, however, that there will be no conflicts. As mentioned earlier, siblings inevitably clash on occasion.

When an adopted child comes first, and then the parents have a biological child, one key problem can stem from thoughtless comments others make. For example, people may tell you it's great you have a child of "your own," which they may say in front of the adopted child. It's important to respond by saying you love both (or all) your children.

This is not to say there are no problems if the biological children enter the family *before* an adopted child. They may become jealous at the extra attention the new kid receives, especially if he's a baby or a toddler. It's probably the same jealousy they'd have if a new baby were born to the family.

So what do you do about it? You say such things as, "Yes, people *are* paying a lot of attention to the new baby. And when you were a baby, people admired you and there were plenty of oohs and ahs—you just can't remember it." If you can think of any anecdotes about what people said or did when your older children were little, it can help your older child feel special. You should also point out that when Baby is the same age as your older child is now, she won't remember all this special attention either.

Getting out your photos of the older child as a baby or toddler can help too. (Or showing your videos of the older child when young.)

When You Have More Than One Adopted Child

Sometimes external factors can complicate your life when you have adopted children with different parents. For example, if you have one adopted child who was adopted in a confidential ("closed") adoption or from an orphanage, with no information on her birth parents, and you have another child who's in an open relationship with her birth parents, sometimes the children will compare what each one has.

The child with the open adoption can know and talk about her birth parents, and won't have to bother with searching for birth parents when she grows up. But as she grows, on some occasions the child from an open adoption may wish she had *fewer* parents to offer opinions on her clothes and hair or her music and desire for a tattoo.

If a Child Thinks Mom (or Dad) Loves Him Best—or Least

When there are two or more children, I can almost guarantee at least at one point, they'll each think Mom or Dad loves them best or least. The trick is to avoid letting this stated perception become a way to manipulate you. "Mom, you never let me go out in cars with my friends, but you always let Judy! You love her best." Never mind that Judy is eighteen and Sandra, the complaining child, is thirteen. Sandra is clearly too young to be going out in cars at night.

Often you can't prove that you're treating your children as fairly as you can, and can only do your best. However, before discounting what the complaining child says, think about it. Sometimes parents *are* harder on some children than others and need to ease off. If, upon reflection, you find it's not true in your case, then don't worry about it.

Coping with Common Problem Behaviors

Most children with a sibling have learned some manipulative behaviors, which parents need to see through. Here are some obvious ways siblings clash in which they involve their parents, and each issue is discussed separately after this list.

- Perceived differences of privileges (You always let her/him do that and I never can.)
- Perceived differences of parental attention (You went to his softball game but you won't go to my dance recital.)

- Perceived differences of punishment (You grounded me for that but you didn't punish her.)

Perceived Differences of Privileges

In most cases, your children are different ages, and generally will have different privileges, usually based on their age, but sometimes taking into consideration their capabilities; for example, you may not let a developmentally delayed adolescent diagnosed with fetal alcohol syndrome stay out until midnight even though his younger brother may stay out late for special occasions.

Understand that no matter how exquisitely fairly you have set privileges for your children, there will be some times when they will be sure they're being mistreated, and they'll let you know about it too. Listen to their viewpoint, because occasionally they may be right. But if not, tell the child you hear his objection and concern, but you don't agree and you're not going to change your rules on privileges.

Perceived Differences of Parental Attention

Sometimes one child will get more attention than another child, either because of very good or very bad behavior. In addition, sick children are more likely to receive attention than well children. It can be difficult, but try to give all your children special time alone with you. You don't want your well-behaved children to get the idea that they have to act up to get some attention, nor do you want your healthy children to conclude that being sick is what gets noticed.

Perceived Differences of Punishment

Your children may believe the parental scales of justice weigh more favorably toward their sibling. In fact, it's not unusual for two children to each think their parents are meaner to them. If a child complains that he's being punished more harshly than his sibling is, consider the complaint seriously because it may be valid. But if it's not fair, tell the child that, for example, because he's older, he's expected to take more responsibility than his little brother. Make sure to remind the child about the privileges that he receives as a benefit for being an older child.

Making Some Basic Rules

It's a good idea to create basic rules for your children regarding their siblings. If they're old enough to read, you can post the rules on the refrigerator or at another common area. If they're not old enough to read, write the rules down and periodically read them to your children. If they break the rules, give a consequence appropriate to the child's age.

Some possible rules might include the following:

- No hitting, biting, slapping, or otherwise physically hurting each other.
- Mom and Dad don't assume that the youngest child or the one who is crying is always innocent.
- No insulting siblings in front of other people.
- Don't take toys, clothes, or other items that belong to someone else without asking for permission first.
- If children divide food, the one who cuts the cake can't choose his piece. (You'll never see such precise division as when a sibling gets to pick the bigger piece.)

Thinking About Adopting Another Child?
Issues to Consider

If you're considering adopting another child, it's important to consider how an adoption might affect children already in your family. Of course you can never know for sure what will happen, but there are some aspects you should think about.

- Do you want to adopt a child who's older or younger than children already in the family? This is important, because it will change the family dynamics. That isn't necessarily bad or good. It's just a factor that needs to be considered.
- Will the new child require a lot of attention (such as a newborn, a child from another country, or a sick child)? If so, think hard about whether you have time to devote to the child.
- Will you expect other children in the family to help? Do *they* have the time or desire to do so?

- Are you adopting another child because you want another child or primarily to supply a playmate for a child already in your home?

Changing Birth Order

If your child is used to running the show because he's the star as an only child, it's only natural there'll be some jealousy about the new intruder, no matter how well it's hidden from your view. Assume that it's there and work with it. You can bring up the topic yourself and see what kind of response you get. If your "old" child bursts into tears or behaves emotionally, you know you need to discuss it with him further.

Potential Needs of the New Child

Consider whether the child to be adopted will have any special needs. If you plan to adopt a child with a disability, you're not the only family member who'll be affected by the new child. If your child is of the same race as you are and you're thinking about adopting a child of a different racial or ethnic background, your "old" child will be affected too, and need to cope with racist remarks and behaviors from others. You may see this as a good learning experience, but it can also be a painful one.

Your Expectations of Your Children If You Adopt Again

Think about accommodations you'll expect from the children already in your family. For example, will a child with her own room be expected to share her room with a new child? In that case, you should discuss it with the child ahead of time. Will you assume your teenager will babysit a toddler when you need time off? If so, have you discussed this with her before telling the social worker, sure, Lindsey would be happy to babysit whenever needed? If not, it's important to do so.

Adopting for Yourself

Some parents say they adopted a second child primarily so the first child will have a sibling. This is not a good main reason to adopt. In one extreme case, a woman adopted an eleven-month old child so her three-year-old would have a sister. The three-year-old detested the younger child. Against the wishes of her husband and her older son, and after the younger child was in the home for a few months, the mother insisted on disrupting the adoption of the younger child. The family was so upset, it seemed unlikely the marriage would last. It was also unfair to the three-year-old child to give her veto power over having a sibling. This example illustrates the folly of adopting a child only to give a sibling to another child.

Joyous Experiences

I've talked about sibling rivalries and conflicts brothers and sisters have with each other. But this isn't the whole picture. There are also joys siblings gain from each other. There's the joy of playing together, and learning new skills from an older brother or sister. There's the fun of laughing and joking with someone in your family who really understands you and thinks you're okay. There's the reliability that if anyone outside the family is harassing a child, a sibling is usually among the first people to defend her. In addition, when the siblings grow to adulthood the close bonds will usually continue, and your children will have in each other lifelong relatives and friends.

Part III

TALKING ABOUT ADOPTION

II

Explaining Adoption to Your Child and to Other Children

ADOPTION MAY SEEM wonderfully and straightforwardly clear to you, and you may feel like it's something that should be easily explained to your child as well—as long as you're completely "open and honest," to use a popular phrase. However, explaining adoption in general to a child, and especially explaining why *your* child was adopted, can be more complicated and confusing than many people think—although of course it's a doable task. (And it's also an ongoing task, because your child will have more questions as she grows older and can better understand such a complex concept as adoption.)

For these reasons, whenever possible, it's important to think ahead about how you'll explain adoption to your children, even before the questions start. And if your child knows she was adopted and is already old enough to ask questions (usually around school age), but isn't asking you anything about her adoption, don't assume she has no questions. Many children have at least a few things that they wonder about with regard to their own adoption, as well as adoption in general.

Keep in mind that you can never be entirely prepared for every question your child might ask you about adoption. But in this chapter, I offer advice on the key issues about adoption that are most commonly asked by children. If you provide your child with this information, you may forestall further questions, although of course that should not be your primary goal. Remember, being asked questions doesn't mean you have failed. It means that you have a curious child, and in most cases that's a good thing. It also means that your child feels comfortable asking you questions, also a positive situation.

Even if you've already explained adoption to your child, this chapter may help you. You can't explain adoption just once and assume that's it, we're done here. Some parents have said with frustration and quite seriously that they told Jacob or Kendra all about adoption when the child was three and now he or she is age six and is entirely clueless about the subject. Think about it: is it sensible to assume small children would remember what you said back when they were toddlers? No, it's not. Your young child may not remember what you said yesterday or last week, let alone three years ago.

Another point about explaining adoption is that, as with explaining to children about sex, religion, or other complex topics, what you tell a three-year-old is far simpler than what you tell a six-year-old or a sixteen-year-old. Children understand abstract concepts at their own developmental level. Children are not just like adults, only smaller. Their thinking abilities and especially their abilities to understand abstract concepts grow as they grow older.

It's also a good idea, if you are involved in a life relationship with another person, to talk to your partner about how you'd like to explain adoption to your child, so you can have a united front. You may also wish to discuss how you plan to explain (or have explained) adoption to other people in your life, a topic covered in the next chapter. (This chapter tells how to explain adoption to other children in and out of your family.)

This chapter also describes common mistakes adoptive parents make when explaining adoption to their children, such as the often-heard "your birth mother placed you for adoption because she loved you." If you take that statement at its face value, as many children do, it sounds like love means inevitably sending people away and saying good-bye to them. That's not a good message to convey to your child about adoption, and I'll explain this issue further in this chapter.

Talking About Adoption with Your Child

Most children want to know what adoption means, and more particularly, why *they* were adopted. If you don't talk about adoption with them, they may develop pretty strange ideas through programs they see on television, statements other people make, and ideas that pop into their own heads somehow.

It's best to convey the idea that adoption is not a perfect answer but it's a solution to problems that sometimes prevent parents from raising children who are born to them. Adoption is also a good way for children to have permanent families. Adoption is not something adoptive parents, adopted children, or birth parents should be ashamed of or apologetic about—although sometimes society in general seems confused about this point.

Remember, as the parent you are your child's primary advocate in life. Sometimes this may include explaining or even defending the institution of adoption itself.

This section breaks down key adoption issues into questions a child might wonder about, and offers you answers you can consider giving your child, keeping in mind that you should personalize your explanation to your own child's situation.

I'd also like to add here that there's no perfect time to tell your child about adoption, so don't wait for one. Make a time, preferably a time when things are calm. Also, if you've delayed telling your child about being adopted and your child is six or seven or older, it's not a disaster and it's not too late. It's easier to tell younger children who are very accepting, but it's still important to tell your older child about adoption. Many people delay talking about adoption for too long, waiting for the perfect time that never comes. Then the child finds out from someone else and feels very betrayed. It's best if the child hears from you that he was adopted.

What Is Adoption?

Tell your child that adoption means that birth parents couldn't handle the job of parenting and that adoptive parents are people who really want to be parents and are approved by other people (such as social workers) to be the permanent and forever parents of the child. That is what happened in your child's case.

Why Was I Adopted?

After telling your child she was adopted, the first and most obvious question is this: Why was your child adopted? Take into account your child's age, and answer this question simply. (Further details are provided in the tips on explaining, later in this chapter.) If the child wants more details, she'll ask for them. If you start providing lots of data and the child gets fidgety and wants to go do something else, you've probably overexplained. Don't worry about it, if that happens. The next time you talk about adoption with your child, you'll know to keep it simple.

One good way to explain why your child was adopted is to explain why most children in general are adopted and then move on to the specifics of why your own child was adopted. The main reason why most children are adopted is because their birth parents were unable to care for them. It's also true that sometimes someone else decided the birth parents were not able to parent the child, such as when the state removes children from families because of abuse or neglect they've inflicted on the child. But the abuse problem is also umbrellaed under the fact that the birth parents were unable to parent the child.

This reason—that some parents are unable to manage parenthood— encompasses the gamut of reasons why children are placed for adoption, including a birth parent's desire for a child to have a stable family, as well as possible struggles with drug abuse or mental illness, physical abuse, and poverty.

Sometimes birth parents don't directly choose adoption by going to see a social worker at an adoption agency or by contacting an adoption attorney. In many countries, the only way for a child to be adopted is for the biological mother to abandon the child anonymously. But if the child was abandoned at or near a hospital or an orphanage, the probable intent of the mother was that others would care for the child, and adoption may also have been on her mind. Again, this mother felt unable to care for her child because of her own personal situation, whether her key problem was poverty combined with social disapproval, or another reason or combination of reasons.

Consequently, when you tell your child why she was adopted, whatever the specific reason was (if you know it), the general reason was an inability to be a parent. This explanation will suffice for most preschoolers, while older children will want more details. Explaining adoption at different ages is addressed later in this chapter.

Why Did *You* Adopt *Me*?

After discussing why the birth mother (and sometimes the birth father was involved with this decision too) chose adoption, the next obvious question is, Why did *you* adopt me? Following are some answers to that question.

Why Families Adopt in General

As with explaining why children are adopted, in explaining why people want to adopt children, you may wish to discuss in general terms why most people adopt a child, and then segue into why your family chose adoption.

Most people adopt children because they want a child to love, and want to give that love to a child who needs a family. Adoptive parents may be infertile (as many are), but people don't have to become parents to survive and thrive. Infertile people must really want to be parents to adopt children. If infertility prevented you from being a parent of a child by birth, you can say so, adding that you're really glad adoption allows people to be parents. Avoid giving your child clinical details on your infertility problems. He or she doesn't need them.

In other cases, some parents may be able to have children but choose to adopt a child rather than have a biological child. Maybe they saw a program on TV that depicted poor children in a foreign orphanage or a child in foster care who needs a family, and they were inspired to investigate adoption. You may also have friends or relatives who adopted children, and subsequently decided you'd like to become a parent by adoption.

Some adopters know or assume they could have more children, while others, such as some single adoptive parents, don't really know if they're fertile because they never sought to have a biological child. This is information that, if you wish to share it with your child, is more appropriate to be given to a school-age child or an adolescent.

Can She (My Birth Mother) Come Back and Get Me?

Sometimes children need explanations of adoption because they are worried or confused about aspects of adoption. Psychiatrists report that sometimes adopted children get the idea that their living situation may be precarious, and that their biological parents could come back at any time and demand them back. Children may worry about this possibility whether a child was adopted in an open or "closed" adoption situation.

For example, children may see a television documentary about adoptive parents battling with birth parents over a baby or toddler, and wonder if this situation could happen to them—even if they're twelve years old right now and far from babyhood.

Even if your child doesn't ask you for a definition of adoption, provide one, telling your child adoption is a permanent transfer of parental rights and obligations, and that your child is yours, and this is forever. Also, be sure to tell your child that television shows have programs about situations that are very unusual. If it was normal for adopted children to be removed from their families, television producers wouldn't bother showing it on TV. Your child's birth parents will not be showing up to take her away from you.

What If I Want to See My Birth Parents? Can I?

Your child's curiosity about his birth parents, particularly the birth mother, may become heated. If you honestly tell the child you don't know where his birth mother is (assuming that's true), he may still think you're lying. Parents know a lot, children think, and this is really important information. Therefore, the child may conclude, you must have this information, but you won't share it with me for some reason.

But if your child was abandoned in an orphanage or even if you adopted a baby from the United States, you may not know who or where the birth parents are. In fact, even if the adoption was an open adoption and you and the birth parents know each other's names, that doesn't mean they'll stay in touch with your family forever. Many adoptive parents report a good relationship with birth parents, but the birth parents drift away and communications become less and less frequent, and often stop altogether. This can be distressing to the child and to the adoptive parents.

Your child may also ask you if he can ever meet his birth parents. If you have a confidential adoption, you don't know the birth parents' identities. However, it may be possible for your child, usually as an adult, to meet his birth parents. Most states in the United States have "mutual consent registries," which means if both the adopted adult and birth parent register, the agency (usually a state agency) will provide identifying information. A few states have "open records," which means the adopted adult may request and be given his original birth certificate, listing the names of his birth parents. There are also organizations such as the International Soundex Reunion Registry in Nevada that help adopted adults worldwide seek out birth parents.

If your child was born in another country, and especially if she was abandoned as an infant, it may be extremely difficult to seek out the birth parents. It's important to realize that unwed motherhood is still considered shameful in many countries.

The key is to tell your child (assuming this is true) that when he's an adult, you'll try to help him identify and locate his birth parents, but you cannot promise to succeed. The fact that you're willing to help can be very reassuring to your child, even though he may be frustrated at having to wait until whatever age a state may require to allow registration on a mutual consent registry.

Was It My Fault?

Another common underlying fear is that adoption was somehow a child's fault. Sometimes children conclude they were adopted because there was something wrong with them. They weren't pretty enough or smart enough, or something else made their birth parents reject them. This fear is so common that you should bring it up at least once, even if your child never mentions it to you.

For example, you might say to your child that sometimes children think it was somehow their fault they were adopted, but it's really the decision of adults to have a child adopted. This decision is made because the birth parent feels unable to be a parent.

If your child is concerned, she'll question you further. Of course, sometimes children will ruminate about what you tell them, and then, days or weeks later, they may ask you about the same topic again.

If your child thinks (or knows) he was adopted to save your marriage, and then your marriage failed anyway, be sure to tell the child it wasn't his fault. Don't overexplain and don't get into details about why your marriage failed unless you must. (For example, if one partner was unfaithful to another partner, that's not an issue most children need details on.)

Note: If your marriage or another long-term relationship failed, be careful about telling children that sometimes people fall "out of love." Your child may wonder if you will stop loving her too. Be sure to emphasize to the child that no matter what happens, you will always love your child and this parent-child relationship will endure.

If Your Child Is Disabled

As discussed in the previous section, sometimes children think they were adopted because they were somehow defective, especially when a child is disabled. She may think she was adopted because her birth mother didn't want a sick child.

Although it's true that some parents place their children for adoption because of the child's developmental delays or physical or emotional problems, it's important to emphasize to your child that the problem was that the birth parents were unable to raise the child, and it was not the child's fault. It can be tricky to avoid blaming birth parents, when you feel your child is wonderful and good parents wouldn't have chosen adoption. Remember that it's best for a child to be parented by someone else if a birth parent feels unable or unready to be a good parent.

If Your Child's Race or Ethnicity Is Different from Yours

Many families adopt children whose racial or ethnic background is different from the adoptive parents' racial or ethnic background. The child may have been adopted from another country, or he could have been adopted from the United States. Fairly early on, around age three or four years old (or even younger), children start to notice it if they don't look just like you.

Don't deny that your child is racially or ethnically different. It's not a sensible thing to do. Instead, tell the child he's Chinese, African-American, Mexican-American, or whatever race or ethnicity is applicable. Tell him his skin color is beautiful. Explain that people of all races are adopted, and adoption isn't about skin color. It's about biological parents who were unable to raise children.

Understand that your child may face troubling questions as he grows up in a transracial family, but in some cases it won't be an adoption issue, but rather a racial issue. (Read more about transracial adoptions in Chapter 15.)

Tips on Talking to Your Child About Adoption

Here are some basic tips to keep in mind as you explain adoption to your child, along with dos and don'ts.

Keep It Simple

When talking to your child about adoption, keep your explanation as simple as possible. For example, explain that the birth mother couldn't take care of her child for some reason, so another parent takes over the job. Many adoptive parents overexplain and provide too many details. If your child wants more information, she'll ask for it.

Don't Explain When You're Overtired or Upset

If your child asks you a question about adoption and you're not prepared to answer the question right then because you're upset, overtired, or something else is distracting you, tell the child you can't answer that question now but you'll answer it later. And then do that: answer the question soon, when things are calmer for you. Don't assume or hope the child will forget she asked you a question. She usually won't forget, and if you never answer the question, she'll deduce that you forgot or you're purposely withholding information. Don't make that mistake.

Don't Depict Birth Parents as Saints

A very common error of social workers is to advise parents to tell their children that they were adopted because their birth mother was such a good and wonderful person. She may actually have been a wonderful person. But that is not why she chose adoption. She chose adoption because she couldn't or didn't wish to be a parent, for a myriad of reasons. This explanation falls along with the "your birth mother loved you, so she had you adopted" explanation discussed later in this chapter, and it's equally invalid and wholly inadequate.

It's okay to say the birth mother was a good person and you admired her (or still do) and other positive comments. But avoid "overselling" the birth mother as the world's greatest person. As with all humans, she was fallible. In her case, she tried to do the right thing. And you're very glad that she did.

Don't Be Negative About the Birth Parents

Although it's not a good idea to depict a child's birth parents as saintly beings (because if they're so wonderful, why did they choose adoption—is what children will ask themselves), it's important to avoid being negative. This doesn't mean you should condone physical abuse, drug abuse, alcoholism, or other problems that sometimes lead children to be adopted.

You can be negative about *behaviors* that are problematic, and that's okay. But you should not be negative about the birth parents themselves. This can be very hard sometimes, especially if you feel the birth parent's behavior was questionable or even bad, and if you feel negatively toward the birth parent. Or maybe abuse wasn't a factor in your child's case, and you adopted him as a newborn. When you've wanted a child for a long time, perhaps years, it can be hard to be philosophical about a fertile woman who willingly chose adoption or who abandoned her child to an orphanage or elsewhere.

The explanation that the birth mother (and often the birth father) was unable to be a parent needs to be one you also accept yourself, even if you have to say it to yourself repeatedly like a mantra.

You may wonder, what does it matter how I feel about the birth parents? It matters because if you feel negatively about the birth parents, and make sarcastic or negative comments about them, your child may eventually think that since he has their genes, maybe he's "bad" too. This is not a concept you want to convey to your child. So if you sense negative comments bubbling up to the surface, count to ten, hold your breath or take some other action. But don't say them. And if you say them anyway, correct yourself when you cool down. Explain sometimes people can't be parents and need other people to adopt children, and you're so glad that you were able to fill that role.

Answer the Questions That Are *Asked*

Listen to what your child asks you before you rush in with explanations. An example of a classic error is seen with the child whose eyes glazed over because he asked where he came from, and his mother gave a detailed description of how much they wanted to adopt, how they found Johnny, and on and on. But Johnny only wanted to know where he was from. Chicago? Los Angeles? Don't assume that all the questions a child may ask about adoption are hard to answer. Some are quite easy to answer.

Be Quiet When the Child Loses Interest

After you've finished your explanation about adoption, stop talking and wait for any questions your child may have. You can also ask if she has any questions. Sometimes the child doesn't, and that's okay. It doesn't mean you did a bad job of explaining, if your child has no questions. Maybe you did a very good job, and that's why she can't think of anything else to ask. Or maybe she needs to think about what you said and will ask you questions later on.

Some Questions Can't Be Answered

Sometimes your child will ask you a question about adoption that you don't want to answer or cannot answer. If you don't know the answer, it's okay to say you don't know. If you know, but don't want to provide further details, simply say it's something you can't discuss now. Every child hates being told that he will understand better when he grows up. But sometimes it's really true.

Talking to Other Children (Including Siblings) About Adoption

Sometimes you'll need to talk to other children about adoption. This situation usually arises when your child has told other children about her adoption and they have questions. Whenever possible, talk to your child first about what she'd like you to tell other children, such as that sometimes birth parents can't parent their children and need someone else to be the parents. See if your child is comfortable with you giving that explanation to her friends. Or, if your child springs it on you, as sometimes happens, give a simple explanation.

Deanna was in the car with her friends, all ages ten and eleven, when she suddenly announced to Mom, who was driving, "Mom, tell them I really *was* adopted!" Mom's on the spot here, but she should not deny the adoption. She can simply say, "Yes, Deanna was adopted as a little baby, and I'm lucky to be her mother."

As Your Child Grows Older

When your child is younger, she may wish to tell the world everything about her adoption, such as how old she was when adopted, where she came from (whether it's Glen Oaks Hospital or a Chinese orphanage), what clothes she wore when you first met her, and so on. Remember, whatever you tell your preteen child, and especially your preschooler, about adoption is likely to be repeated to the world at large. This is one reason to avoid telling a young child about very harsh realities, such as that she was abandoned or that her birth mother was raped.

As your child grows older, she may become more reticent about what she wants other children to know about her adoption or even to know that she was adopted. Periodically revisit with your child how she wants you to handle explanations about adoption with other children.

As with your own child, other small children outside your family are usually satisfied with simple details, while older children, especially adolescents, may be far more probing. You don't have to answer questions if you don't wish to and especially if you feel it would be embarrassing to your child.

When You Have Other Adopted Children

If you adopt more than one child, each child's adoption will be somewhat different, even if you adopted them from the same city or country. The child who's already in the family will want to know why you're adopting another child. He may also secretly wonder if he wasn't enough for you, so you had to go and find someone better. Tell your child who was first in your family that you love him very much and there's room in your heart for more than one child. (This is also a good thing to tell your nonadopted children.)

Before the new child comes, you can talk about how your first child came into your family and how excited you and your spouse or life partner were on that special day. Keep in mind that there's always a little jealousy when a new family member comes, but try to continue to make special time for the child or children who were first in your life, including after the newly adopted child comes home to your family.

If You Have Nonadopted Children

If you have other children who were not adopted, they need to learn about adoption in an age-appropriate manner. Don't assume your older children will somehow know why you adopted a child. Tell them.

Lori says one day Josh, age ten, told her that he was sorry he had ripped up her insides before he got born so she couldn't have more babies after him and had to adopt Jacob. Lori was astonished and speechless. She assured Josh her infertility was not his fault at all, and she was happy she had Josh and later adopted Jacob. Lori thought about the situation and remembered talking to her sister on the phone, telling her she had wanted more children after Josh, but her uterus had been badly damaged and she had to have a hysterectomy, so she had to adopt a child if she wanted more children. Lori was certain she had never "blamed" Josh for this medical problem, either on the phone or in her own mind. But apparently Josh had heard Lori's conversation and had come to that wrong conclusion. (Lori's now more circumspect about what she says on the phone when her children are present.)

Be careful what you tell siblings about a newly adopted child. For example, if the birth mother of your adopted child had problems with alcohol or drug abuse, this isn't information siblings need to know, at least until they are older. No matter how loving and caring you think your nonadopted child is, sometimes siblings get angry with each other, and may use whatever ammunition they have. If it's something bad about a birth mother, it may get flung out like a verbal rock in an angry moment. So don't provide any potential rocks in the first place. (Read more about sibling relationships in Chapter 10.)

Common Mistakes About Explaining That Adoptive Parents Make

You'll never explain adoption to your child in a perfect way, but here are some common mistakes many adoptive parents make. Sometimes social workers and others may encourage you to make some of these mistakes: resist them if that happens.

Your Birth Mother Chose Adoption Because She Loved You

I still sometimes hear about advice from social workers and others who tell adoptive parents to explain adoption to their children by saying their birth mother chose adoption because she loved them and leave the explanation at that.

The problem with saying a child's birth mother chose adoption solely because she loved him or her is that children think very simplistically. It's also a very abstract notion to think of someone acting unselfishly for the good of her child, although that may well be true of your child's birth mother. But the fact is that she didn't place the child for adoption only because she loved him. She chose adoption for another reason altogether.

Maybe she chose adoption because she felt she was too young to be a mother or because she was single and she wanted the child to have a two-parent family. Maybe she felt unable to raise the child because of emotional problems. There are many reasons why women choose adoption. But to say love is the sole reason makes little sense to a child. After all, *you* love your child too, don't you? Does that mean that you might have her adopted at some point in the future? Of course it doesn't. But children can easily assume it might mean this, when you use love as the sole reason for an adoption occurring.

Instead of using the "your mother loved you so much that she chose adoption for you" explanation, emphasize instead that the birth mother felt unable to parent her child. You can still incorporate the love aspect by saying that the birth mother chose adoption as a loving option, since she was unable to parent her child.

You Were Adopted Because Your Family Was Poor

The explanation that the child was adopted because his birth parents were poor may be valid, especially when the child was adopted from another country. But it's a bad idea to attribute the entire adoption to poverty. There are always other reasons as well. For example, a woman in another country who is pregnant out of wedlock may be shunned by her family and by others in the country. This is a cultural problem in addition to a poverty problem.

In the United States, there are systems set up to help people who are poor and to provide at least temporary financial assistance. Your child may realize this and wonder why his birth mother didn't seek financial help. You may not know why, although there are plenty of ways you could speculate. Some women in the United States don't like to apply for public assistance or, as it was formerly called, "go on welfare." And women in some other countries may not have the option of using public assistance and parenting their child, because there are no social supports available to them in that country.

Another problem with the poverty explanation is that the child may start worrying someday if you should start to complain about bills piling up and if you tell your child that you're not "made of money." If poverty was the cause for his being adopted, does that then mean then that if *you* have financial problems, he'll be placed for adoption again? If your child is a preadolescent, he may wonder and worry about this.

As a result, it's okay to say that poverty was *part* of the reason for your child's being placed for adoption. But it wasn't the only reason. If you use the poverty explanation, be sure to tell your child that no matter how poor you might ever become, even if you lost all your money, he'll still be your child and you'll find a way to support him. This is a permanent relationship, and you need to make that very clear.

God Decided You Should Be Adopted

Many people think that their children came to them either directly or indirectly as a result of an act of God. They may think that this is a perfect explanation of adoption. But one problem with this explanation is that, again, it's incomplete. You don't really know that God told the birth mother that she should have her child adopted, and you don't know that other actions took place as a result of the actions of God.

If you use the "God did it" explanation, combine it with the motivation behind the human birth mother, as far as you know it. She felt unable to be a parent. You can still incorporate God into your explanation by speculating that perhaps God showed the birth mother the way to adoption when she felt unable to parent her child, and that is why the child was adopted.

The Chosen Child Mistake

Another common mistake is to tell a child she was particularly *chosen* for adoption. She may think she has some kind of special markings on her, visible only to you and a few others. Saying a child was chosen for adoption may, on the surface, seem like a nice thing to say. But it can put an unreasonable burden on a child, to feel she must be especially good to be worthy, since she was chosen. Also, in most cases, the chosen child story isn't true at all. The adoption agency usually helped you find your child.

However, if you really did select the child from photographs of waiting children or in some other way you actually did choose the child, it can be a nice story for the child to hear. It's important, however, to make sure that the "chosen child" explanation isn't all that the child hears, so that she feels she somehow owes her life to you and must be extra-special good to be worthy of having been adopted. The other part of the equation, and one that should never be ignored, is that the birth parents were unable to parent the child.

If You Don't Know Why Your Child Was Placed for Adoption

In some cases, you don't know why your child was placed for adoption. Maybe your child came from another country and was abandoned at an orphanage, and that's all you know. Maybe your child came from the United States and was placed for adoption, but the birth mother provided few details to the attorney or adoption agency about her circumstances or why she placed her child for adoption.

When you aren't really sure why a child was placed for adoption (or abandoned), there's one simple explanation that covers all situations, and it's the one already mentioned several times: the biological parents were unable to care for the child. This explanation covers any situation you can imagine, including abusive behavior, alcoholism, drug addiction, poverty, and so on.

Explaining Adoption to Your Child at Different Ages

As mentioned at the beginning of this chapter, you can't expect to explain adoption to your child the same way when she's little as when she's a school-age child or an adolescent. Instead, it's best to build on earlier explanations.

When is it a good idea to start explaining adoption? In most cases, the explanation should occur before the child enters school. Some parents attempt to explain adoption to their children when they're three or four years old, generally the earliest ages at which children can have the most rudimentary understanding of adoption. Other parents wait until the child is five or six years old, which is usually just fine. Keep in mind, however, that sometimes neighbors or relatives may mention the adoption to the child, assuming that she already knew about it.

As for repeatedly saying to your infant, "You're my beautiful adopted baby," I do not recommend this. Babies need love, care, and attention, and can't possibly understand the word "adoption." They can barely understand "Mama" or "Dada." The only person who pays attention when the phrase "my beautiful adopted baby" is repeatedly stated is the person saying it, and many experts believe this is an alienating thing for the adoptive parent to say, rather than a positive statement.

Explaining Adoption to Small Children

If you decide to explain adoption to a small child of three to five years old (or you *need* to explain adoption because your child is of a different race or ethnicity than you), keep your explanation very simple. The birth mother was unable or unready to be a parent. However, and very fortunately, you were ready and able to raise a child.

Many small children love to hear the story of when you first saw them in the hospital, the agency office, the orphanage, or wherever. They like to hear about what happened when you drove home or flew home on the airplane with the child, and how you were so excited and sleepless when your new child came home for the first time. You may have to tell the "adoption story" over and over to your child.

Make sure you tell your small child that he or she was born. It sounds ridiculous to most adults, but some children hear so many stories about the plane ride or the orphanage or wherever their parents first met them that they can get the strange idea they were not actually born like other children. Tell them all children are born to a mother and sometimes that mother can't take care of them. When that happens, another mother (and/or father) takes care of them. It's called "adoption," and you are that person who was the adopter.

Small children usually don't have many questions about adoption, and they generally accept whatever you tell them. They also think adoption must be good because you think it's good, although they can't possibly grasp what adoption is. A small child may be sad to learn that he didn't "grow in your tummy," and you can say that this makes you sad too, but you still love him the same.

Explaining to School-Age Children

Adoption gets trickier to explain as children get older. The happy adoption story often no longer is enough, and the school-age child will want to know *why* a birth parent felt unable to raise him. If you have an open adoption, your child may ask both you and the birth parent many difficult questions. If you have a confidential adoption, the child may find it hard to believe that you don't have much information about his birth parents. However, if you're being candid, he'll eventually realize that this is the truth.

When your child is school-age, it's also a good idea to tell your child that sometimes others don't really "get" adoption. They may confuse it with temporary parenting, or they may think that all adopted children come from other countries or from the United States. There are many wrong ideas that others may have, and it's a good idea to alert your child to this fact. Emphasize that adoption is a permanent family obligation of the parents, and that you chose it willingly and lovingly and you're very glad that you did.

School-age children may still have trouble understanding why anyone would choose to have her child adopted. Face it: it's hard for many adults to understand the same thing, so it's not surprising that children struggle with this concept. If your child feels sad in thinking about not being able to stay with his birth mother, this is a normal feeling and not a renunciation of you and your love.

You may also find that although adoption was readily accepted in the past, the school-age child may have more questions. Preadolescents may learn about genetics and sometimes may even be given a project such as a family tree to draw. Some children simply use their adoptive parents as the "limbs" of the tree, while others are torn about what to do about the family tree exercise. (See Chapter 8 for more on this issue.)

You can also tell your older child that a social worker and a judge in a court approved the adoption. (Sometimes children get odd ideas about being "stolen" from their biological parents.) Your school-age child may wish to see the adoption decree, which should be okay. Don't let the child take it out of the house to show her friends, however, because it might get lost or damaged. Explain to your child that the adoption decree is an important legal document that needs to be kept in your home with your other important papers.

Explaining Adoption to Adolescents

It's probably the toughest to talk with teens about their adoption. Teenagers are on their way to adulthood, but they can be very judgmental. They may think their birth parents must have been bad to not have been able to care for them. Teenagers will also often need to be reminded that it wasn't their own fault they were adopted. Often the decision to place a child for adoption was made while the birth mother was still pregnant.

Tell your adolescent that in a perfect world, all parents would raise the children that were born to them. But this is *not* a perfect world, and sometimes it's better for children to be adopted by other people. Also tell your child that you're very happy that you had the opportunity to adopt him or her. Adolescents need to hear this, because often parents complain (and rightfully so!) about teenage behaviors.

Understand that your teenager is going through identity conflicts and issues of growing up. In some cases, your child may tell you, quite frankly, that his birth parents would *have* to be better than you, because you're a terrible parent. It hurts to hear such a statement, even though you should know that rarely is it justified. Realize that most nonadopted adolescents also consider their parents hopeless. The adopted adolescent has the extra burden of knowing that he has different parents that he was born to.

It's also common for a teenager to assume his birth parents are wonderful and glamorous people. Your teenager may secretly imagine that his birth mother is a famous rock star or a movie personality. Alternatively, some teenagers assume that their birth parents were evil criminals. This is part of the black-and-white/either-or thinking of adolescents—you're either wonderful or you're terrible. It's hard for them to imagine that their birth parents are average people, although in most cases that's what they are.

Key Points to Convey to Your Child

This chapter provides details about various dos and don'ts in explaining adoption to your child. Here are the major "take-home" points:

1. Birth parents choose adoption (or sometimes have it chosen for them, as with foster children removed from their families) because they can't provide the needed parenting. Adoptive parents take on this important job.
2. Birth parents are usually normal people, and not saints or sinners.
3. Adoption is not the child's "fault." Decisions about adoption are nearly always made by adults.
4. Adoptive parents adopt for many different reasons, but the common denominator for nearly all of them is that they want to be parents to a child.
5. Children need adoption explanations appropriate to their age. You can provide more details (if you have them) to an adolescent about his adoption than you'd offer a five-year-old.
6. Explaining adoption is not a one-time task. Children will have more questions as they grow older.
7. Children may be very curious about their adoption, and sometimes it may make them sad. These are nearly always normal feelings.

12

Talking with Others About Adoption

How do you explain adoption to other people, and convey the love and complexity of this institution older than Moses (an adopted person) himself? It's generally not possible for others to fully appreciate adoption the same way that you do, no matter how well you explain adoption to your friends, family members, and others. (Unless they're also adoptive parents.) In addition, even if you're exceptionally good at explaining adoption, some people will cling to wrong and stupid ideas, such as that adoption is second-class, adopted children weren't wanted children, you "saved" them by adopting, and so on. But if you use the tactics and the explanations provided in this chapter, adjusting them to your needs, it's a good start for a common sense parent.

You may also worry about saying the wrong thing or providing not enough or too much information about your child to others. Keep in mind that sometimes no matter how hard you try, your efforts won't work out the way you hoped. The key is to convey what you know about adoption in a positive and realistic manner, with the underlying basic premise that you are your child's best advocate.

This chapter describes how to discuss adoption with relatives and your friends. In addition, it offers advice on talking about adoption with other key people in your child's life, such as teachers, physicians, and others who may affect your child and you.

Providing Basic Information to Others

You may find explaining adoption to others not that difficult, or conversely, it may be trickier than you expected. It depends on how comfortable you feel about talking about the subject, how receptive your listeners are to what you have to say, and even what else is going on at the time. (When you're in the middle of an argument is not a good time to score points on what you know about adoption. For one thing, the person you're talking to is less likely to listen to what you're saying if she's in an angry frame of mind.)

You may be surprised by what others think or say about adoption. For example, many people confuse adoption with foster parenting, while others confuse stepparenting with adoptive parenting. Some people confuse all three forms of parenting with each other, including some newscasters and journalists.

Basic Points to Make About Adoption

There are certain simple facts about adoption that you should share with others, if you talk about adoption at all, and these are as follows:

- Adoption is permanent.
- Adoption is a legal change, involving the court.
- Adoption is another good way to create a family.
- Some aspects of adoption are private.
- Most adopted children grow up to be just fine.

Adoption Is Permanent

Many people don't understand the permanent nature of adoption. Maybe part of the reason is that nearly all states have a period of time between the placement of the child in your family until the finalization of the adoption. During that time adoptive parents feel very anxious, but adoptions rarely fall through after a child is placed with a family. (Sometimes birth mothers "change their minds" before a child is placed.) Tell others adoption is a permanent transfer of parental obligations from one family (usually the birth parents) to another family (yours).

In contrast to adoptive parents, foster parents aren't given the rights and obligations of a parent, because the court hasn't decided whether to return a child to his parents, so it's meant to be a temporary situation. Sometimes foster parents adopt their foster children, if the court decides this would be in the best interest of the child. In that case, their status changes from foster parents to adoptive parents. It really does make a difference to family members once a child is adopted. Many foster children have reported the thrill of having a permanent relationship and the joy they felt in taking on the former foster parents' (now adoptive parents!) last name.

Stepparents are married to other individuals who already have one or more children. Sometimes stepparents adopt their stepchildren. In most states, a stepparent adoption is a much simpler process than a nonrelative adoption is.

If the stepparent formally adopts the child, he or she is transformed into an adoptive parent. Adoption is a serious and important step for a stepparent, indicating he accepts the obligations, joys, and responsibilities of the child. Some people say adopting a stepchild (or a foster child) is comparable to the difference between living with a person and committing to that person in marriage.

Adoption Involves a Court

You should also explain to others that in nearly all states, there is a brief (or sometimes not-so-brief!) period before the adoption is finalized, so the courts can ensure everything is in order. You had to have a study done on your family, sort of like a background investigation, to make sure you were healthy and otherwise fit to adopt. Many people are impressed by the fact that you underwent an investigative process and that a judge finalized your child's adoption in court. (And they should be.)

You may wish to explain that you received an adoption decree, a document affirming your adoption. If people ask to see the adoption decree (usually they won't), it's up to you. Would those same people ask to see your marriage certificate or birth certificate? And if they did, would you be as willing to hunt down that document? Asking yourself such questions may guide you as to whether to show others the adoption decree.

Adoption Is Another Good Way to Create a Family

The two-parent biological family is no longer the norm for many children in our society. People can argue at great length whether this is good or bad, but the fact is that many children now grow up with single parents, stepparents, adoptive parents, relative caregivers such as grandparents, foster parents, and in other types of family arrangements.

This may mean (hopefully) that adoption will become a more accepted way of creating a family than in past years, when some people thought adoption was embarrassing and a secret to be kept since it was perceived as so different from the standard way to form a family. In the past it was considered normal for a man and woman to marry and have 2.3 children born to them. Now many children have "half" siblings as well as siblings that are unrelated to them, whether they were adopted or not.

Some Aspects of Your Child's Adoption Are Private

When you explain adoption to others, you're not required by law or by custom to share everything you know about your child's adoption. In fact, it's generally best if you don't do so. The reason for this advice is the unfortunate tendency among some people to remember with great clarity anything that might possibly be construed as negative, while the positive things that you might say are far too easily forgotten. As a result, it's usually best that you don't tell everyone about every aspect of your child's adoption, although many new parents seem to have a compulsion to do so.

So, for example, if a birth mother was a beautiful concert pianist who spoke five languages, and also had a drug problem, and you told people all this information, which part do you think they'd remember? Sadly, you can count on it that most people will remember the drug problem part, and forget about the beauty or the linguistic or musical skills of the birth mother.

It's also true that some people will assume that if a biological mother had a drug problem, her child is at risk for having the same problem, although most adopted children do not exhibit the same problem behaviors as their biological parents.

Realize and also tell others that some aspects of your child's adoption are private. Don't worry, the Adoption Police will not show up on your doorstep if you refuse to divulge details to others such as how old the birth mother was, if you know who the father was, if your adoption is open, and so forth. You are allowed to keep some or even most details to yourself, although you may wish to share with others your child's name, birth date, and whether she came from Indiana or India—or elsewhere.

Keep in mind, as your child grows up, that although it was fine with her that you shared information about her adoption with others when she was five, and enjoyed hearing how she had such cute little hiccups and was the most adorable thing you'd ever seen in your life, that same child will usually not feel the same way when she's twelve, and definitely not when she's fifteen or sixteen. Talk to your child, and find out what information it's okay to share with others. If your child doesn't want you to talk about her adoption at all to others, honor that request. (Ask again later on, and your child may have changed her mind, allowing a few details to be shared with others.)

Most Adopted Children Grow Up to Be Just Fine

You may also wish to point out to your family, friends, and others that most adopted children grow up to be healthy and normal children, based on studies done by the Search Institute in Minnesota and other organizations. After saying that, you may feel offended if someone says, "I wouldn't adopt because I wouldn't take on someone else's problem." Try to be patient, and explain that you don't regard your child as a "problem," but rather as a blessing. And think to yourself that it's best that people who look down on adopted children *don't* adopt. Imagine how awful it would be for their children!

Count to ten if others say offensive things. You can choose to say nothing, or you can say briefly that you don't agree and then walk away.

What if your child does develop emotional problems or act out and friends and others comment on this? Point out that many nonadopted children also have emotional problems or exhibit bad behavior, primarily in adolescence. And most children, adopted or not, grow out of it.

Relating to Your Relatives

Your parents, siblings, and the relatives of your significant other will play an important role in your child's life, and it can be a very positive role. Rarely, however, some relatives take a negative view of adopted children as "second-class." If that happens, there should be no contest: you're on your child's side. So if Grandma or Aunt Sally fusses over your biological child or your brother's biological child but consistently ignores your adopted child, you'll need to discuss this issue with them. If matters don't improve despite repeated attempts, you may choose to limit your contact with such relatives, for your child's sake. (But be honest: will you really miss such people? Probably not.)

Understand that even though you may wish to keep some aspects of your child's adoption private, people in your family may feel they have the "right" to know everything. Ironically, they are also in the position to cause (usually inadvertently) the worst harm to your child if information you provide to them is negative. Strangers won't care and the supermarket cashier will never ask your growing child if his birth mother got over that bad alcohol problem. But Aunt Sue, after she's had a few drinks, might make such a comment to your distressed teen on New Year's Eve. This is yet another reason to limit negative information that you give your relatives about your child's birth family.

Sometimes relatives may aggravate you, usually unwittingly, by introducing your child as your "adopted daughter" or "adopted son" rather than simply your daughter or son. Take them aside later and tell them you prefer they simply use the term son or daughter. Some people also react with humor by saying, "Yes, and Timmy is Aunt Mary's C-section child," making the point that way. (Avoid embarrassing any children, whenever possible.)

Talking to Friends

True friends care about you, and are likely to believe and support you in what you tell them about adoption in general and your child in particular. A good friend listens to your point of view and respects it. Yet some friends may harbor secret beliefs, such as that biological parenting is always superior, but may not say such annoying things to you.

Your family and friends may develop some odd ideas about what adoption is and may express these ideas to you, in which case you can educate them when they're wrong. They may also keep these thoughts to themselves, but sometimes you can tell that something isn't quite right.

Ask the person what's wrong, and if she has a question that you haven't answered yet. You may find the person is really curious about some aspect of adoption because she wants to adopt a child herself or knows someone who does. In other cases, you may be talking to a birth mother who placed a child for adoption herself many years ago, and is understandably fascinated by your adoption of a child. Sometimes adults who question you were adopted themselves, and just never mentioned it to you before.

Talking to Casual Others (Neighbors or Friendly Strangers)

Sometimes total strangers ask you questions that relate to your child's adoption. Again, remember that when you adopt a child, you don't take an oath that you must tell the world all about your child's birth parents and his adoption. You and your child are entitled to some privacy, and it's your job, as a parent, to protect that privacy.

People who aren't close to you may be very blunt in their questions or may attempt to be tactful. Sometimes even when people think they're being tactful, they may upset you with comments about the "real mother" or "natural mother" instead of the preferable term "birth mother." In most cases, the reason they use such phrases is that they've never heard words like "birth mother" before. Keep that fact in mind.

Don't criticize them for failing to use proper adoption terminology. Instead, use the word "birth mother" or "birth parent" as you talk about adoption. After a while, others will unconsciously mirror your use of the word. If they ask you what exactly a birth mother is, explain that most people interested in adoption call a woman who had a child who was later adopted a birth mother. Others call her a biological mother or a genetic mother, but birth mother seems to be the easiest to understand.

Talking to Teachers, Doctors, and Other Professionals

Here's a group that can intimidate even the most common sense–filled adoptive parent: professionals who are supposed to know what they're talking about when they talk about children, including teachers, physicians, and other professionals you may deal with, such as psychologists and others. It can be daunting to deal with them sometimes.

Most of the time, your relationships with such professionals will be cordial and mutually respectful. Occasionally, you may encounter a problem person who regards adoption through a negative prism and is not about to change his mind. If this person is a teacher, doctor, or someone else who is involved with your child's welfare, then you'll need to take steps to get a different doctor or teacher for your child.

Straight Talk About Teachers

Most teachers are sensitive and caring people. They may know nothing, a
little, or a lot about adoption. They may have negative ideas about adopted
children, such as that they are pathetic beings who must be protected or
that one shouldn't expect too much of them. In short, teachers are like people in the general population in their ignorance about adoption. You
shouldn't assume they understand adoption at all, although they may.

Many parents agonize endlessly over whether they should tell their children's teachers a child was adopted. Sometimes you may feel like there's no real
choice, such as when you adopt a child of another race. Other times, the child
and the parents are the same race and there's no pressing necessity to bring up
adoption, but you may wish to raise the subject anyway. (I discuss the subject
of teachers at greater length in Chapter 8, including the problem of the family tree school exercise and other topics that sometimes distress children.)

Some school registration forms have a block for parents to check if the
child was adopted. What if you don't wish to check that block? My coauthor says she always ignored the adoption block because she felt it was no
one's business that her son was adopted, and no one ever challenged her.

Other parents would go ahead and check an "adopted" block on a school
registration form, and they'd go much further than that. Some parents choose
to create a program about adoption to present to children in their child's preschool or kindergarten class. This can be a charming and positive idea. Children in this age group are very accepting of each other for the most part.

Communicating with Pediatricians and Other Physicians

Doctors tend to be smart people, but sometimes they have biased views
about adoption and adopted children. As a pediatrician who treats many
adopted and nonadopted children, I try to educate other doctors about the
realities of adoption. (Chapter 14 also discusses medical issues related to
adopted children.)

If you have the information, provide specific types of information
about your child to doctors, including the following basics:

- A family history (in the birth family) of serious medical problems
  (allergies, heart disease, diabetes, cancer, kidney disease, or other
  ailments)

- Pregnancy and birth problems a child experienced (prenatal exposure to drugs or alcohol, a difficult delivery, the need for a transfusion or surgery, or other unusual circumstances)
- Neonatal problems (any health problems a child experienced as a newborn baby)
- Immunizations the child has had, if any
- Health problems a child has had to date, if any
- Medications a child has taken, if known, especially if there were reactions

If you adopted an older child (age three or older when the child entered your family), you may have little or no health information on the child, depending on the situation. If the child was a foster child, the state should have medical information on the child, although it may be scanty and difficult to obtain. The social worker may send you records with blocked-out sections, to protect the confidentiality of the biological family. This is okay because you don't need their name to understand medical problems.

If the child lived in an orphanage, the orphanage director should have information on the child from when the child entered the institution to when she left it. Your adoption agency should be able to obtain some of this information for you.

The types of medical information you should obtain on an older child, if possible (in addition to the birth history and other items I've already discussed), are as follows:

- Immunizations the child has had to date (although the doctor may wish to repeat them if they were done in another country)
- Health problems the child has, particularly infectious diseases such as any form of hepatitis or tuberculosis
- Any broken bones or injuries that the child may have experienced
- Any medical evaluations by specialists

If you feel your child's doctor is biased against adoption, ask her about it. Don't say, "Do you hate adopted children?" because the obvious answer is no. Instead, you may wish to ask a question such as, "Some people are troubled by some aspects of adoption. Are there any areas that concern you?" Another question you could ask is, "What has been your experience to date with adopted children in your own practice?"

If you receive a response that really bothers you, indicating a very negative attitude toward adopted children, then you will need to change doctors. You wouldn't want a black child to be seen by a racist physician, and you shouldn't take an adopted child to an anti-adoption doctor.

Talking to Therapists

Most adopted children won't need therapy, but some children experience emotional problems and you'll need to contact a therapist. (Read Chapter 16 for a discussion of emotional problems.) Make sure the therapist doesn't assume all adopted children are emotionally disturbed.

Simply "being adopted" is not a clinical diagnosis, and you need to find another therapist if you receive the impression from the therapist that all adopted children are inherently disturbed by virtue of being adopted. Use your common sense.

13

How and When to Talk About Adoption

TALKING ABOUT ADOPTION to your child and others can be a challenging task. You may feel unsure about what kinds of information you should share, as well as what (if anything) to emphasize. You may worry about how to discuss sensitive topics with your child. You may also wonder about what you should tell others, such as family, friends, your child's teachers, and other individuals. How much information is enough and how much is too much? In addition, should you wait for the right time to bring up the topic or set aside a specific time and plunge in? These topics are addressed in this chapter.

Sample conversations are also offered for you to consider, including conversations between parents and children, a conversation between a parent and a relative, and a conversation between a parent and a teacher. It's important, however, to realize these conversations are in no way meant to be used as scripts. Life is unpredictable and your child (and others) will respond to you in their own unique way. Thus, the conversations are meant to stimulate thought and discussion. I hope they'll also provide you with ideas on how to handle difficult situations you may face.

When to Talk About Adoption—and When Not To

The best times to talk about adoption are when you and your child are in calm moods and undistracted by situations swirling around you. If your life is constantly chaotic with soccer matches, dance classes, your job, and so on, don't wait for the perfect time to talk about adoption (it may never happen!), but choose the least tumultuous time.

Often it seems children bring up difficult questions when you're in a waiting room of a doctor's office or while driving home with them. You're struggling through rush hour traffic on the interstate and your eight-year-old son suddenly wants to know why he was adopted and where are his birth parents. Do you owe him an answer? Sure, but not now, when the safety of you both would be imperiled if you were distracted from driving carefully. In such a situation, you should tell your child that you can't talk now because of the bad traffic but you'll talk to him later tonight or tomorrow. (And keep that promise.)

Libby, who has a twelve-year-old daughter, Ashley, picked a casual Sunday afternoon to discuss Ashley's adoption with her again. (Ashley had known for years that she was adopted as a baby.) Ashley's best friend was sick and it was raining outside. Ashley was obviously bored, so Libby decided this might be a good time to bring up adoption and see if Ashley had any questions about it. Libby's plan was to see if Ashley was interested in talking about the subject. If so, they had time to continue the conversation. If, however, Ashley seemed distractible or clearly not interested, Libby decided in advance that she wouldn't press it. But she would let Ashley know that she could always bring questions or worries to her mother.

Listen to Your Child

One of the toughest parts about explaining adoption to your child (and sometimes to others too) is in listening to what they're actually asking you. This means listening to the words said, but it also means paying attention to the child's tone of voice (anxious, casual, curious, or another tone) as well as to his body language (leaning forward with interest, staring off into space, or standing with arms folded across the chest defiantly). It also means taking into account your child's age and level of understanding. The child's emotional maturity is also important. Consider all these aspects when discussing adoption with your child, as well as other difficult subjects such as sex and religion.

Sample Conversations Between a Parent and Child

Chapter 11 provides advice on talking about adoption to your child at different ages. This section offers conversations that may occur between a parent and a child, in the form of dialogues. Your child may respond differently from the children here, but these conversations can give you ideas on explaining adoption to your child.

In the first conversation, Carla ("Mom") is talking about adoption in general to her daughter Amy, age ten. Amy has told her that she's just seen a made-for-TV movie in which the main characters felt different and weird because they were adopted children. Amy wonders if all adopted children feel like the children in the TV show or if they feel mostly okay about adoption, as Amy does.

AMY: So Mom, do you think I am like, really well-adjusted compared to other kids who are adopted, or am I weirdly different—or what's the deal?

MOM: Amy, I do think you're a very well-adjusted girl! I also don't think it's possible or even fair to lump together all adopted kids into one or two categories, like "well-adjusted" or "not well-adjusted." There are a lot of differences among adopted people.

AMY: Okay, Mom. But who's *more* like most adopted kids? Me or the kids on the TV show?

MOM: I don't know how to answer that, Amy. For the reasons I just gave you. Maybe it would help if you talked to other kids who were adopted and see how they feel about it.

AMY: But I don't *know* any other adopted kids. I think I'm the only one in school. Anyway, how could I ever find anybody who was adopted? Besides, I don't want to talk to anyone who might be crazy or awful.

MOM: Amy, I know enough about adoption to tell you most adopted kids aren't crazy or awful. That's a stereotype, like that all Korean kids are great at math! As for finding them, I'm sure there are adopted kids around here. We just don't happen to know who they are. If we ask around, we could find them. Or maybe you could talk to some adopted adults about how they feel about adoption. Of course, I'd have to meet them first, to make sure they're okay people for you to hang out with.

AMY: I have trouble with math and I'm Korean! Why would anyone think Asians are extra good at math? That is so dumb! Could I find some adopted kids on the Internet? Maybe that would work.

MOM: Most adopted adults are normal people, Amy, but I don't want you to be talking to any adult whom I haven't personally met myself! You know that's the way I am. It's not about adoption, it's about your personal safety.

AMY: Okay. But what about the Internet thing? Could I meet someone that way?

MOM: That might work, Amy. One possible problem is some adopted people on the Internet are looking for others to complain to about how terrible their lives are. Some people blame all their problems in life on being adopted.

AMY: I don't do that! And I wouldn't do that.

MOM: No, you've got a good head on your shoulders, Amy. Maybe we could find an adoptive parent group with members who have kids your age. Sometimes those groups have picnics or parties that the whole family attends.

AMY: Are they mostly kids adopted from Korea, like me?

MOM: Probably they're kids adopted from Korea, the United States, and lots of other countries. We could check around. There's also "culture camps" of kids adopted from other countries, where kids meet each other and can learn about the countries where they were born. That might be fun for you. I read about it in *Adoptive Families* magazine.

AMY: Wow, let me think about that more. Could I read the article too? Thanks, Mom!

Here's another conversation with a less-happy adolescent, Frank, age fourteen, and his father.

FRANK: Why did you adopt me anyway? All I do is work, work, work. Did you adopt me so that I could be your personal slave or something? My real parents wouldn't make me do all these chores all the time!

DAD: Frank, I'm trying to hold my temper here. No, I did not adopt you to have a "personal slave," as you put it. If I had, those first years when you were small were a total waste! What I've asked you to do is no different than what other families have their children do, like take out the trash, pick up your room, and mow the lawn once a week. That's also, by the way, why you receive an allowance.

FRANK: Okay, but if we were rich, I wouldn't have to do these chores! What if my birth mother, as you call her, were rich? That's possible, isn't it? I would have such an easy life!

DAD: As far as I was told, your birth parents were not rich. In fact, most birth parents are average people. They're not rich socialites and they're not homeless people living in boxes, either. So if you hadn't been adopted, you'd probably *still* have to do chores, maybe lots more of them, for all I know!

FRANK: I just feel like sometimes you don't appreciate me like the way you would if I was born to Mom. I bet you'd treat your real son way different from me. Way better!

DAD: Frank, you are my real son. You were adopted, but I love you the same as if you were born to Mom. I can't prove to you I'd treat a biological child the same as you, since you're the only child I have. I'm just telling you I know in my heart that it's true.

FRANK: Well, okay, but how come you never bring up my being adopted and you don't seem to want to talk about it much? Was my real mother a drug addict or maybe was my real father a drug lord or something like that?

DAD: I have plenty of things to think about, Frank! And I don't have that much information on your birth parents. What I have, I've given you. I'm pretty sure they were not drug addicts or drug lords! From what your mother tells me, a lot of adopted kids think their biological parents are either saints or very bad people. I guess that would make it more exciting and dramatic. But it's just not that way in your case and in the case of most other adopted kids.

FRANK: Well, do you think they ever think about me, Dad?

DAD: I can't say for sure, but I think they probably do, maybe on your birthday or at other times. They may hope and pray that you're healthy and happy.

FRANK: Maybe when I'm older, I'll want to meet them and show them that I'm okay and see what they're like too.

DAD: That could probably be arranged, although I don't know exactly how, but Mom and I would help you all we could, when the time comes. But you have to be at least eighteen before we start something like that.

FRANK: Okay. Can you drive me to the mall now? And can we pick up Carol and Jimmy on the way too? They need rides.

Discussing Adoption with Others

Sometimes it can be challenging to talk to family members and friends about adoption, and they may make remarks that can set your teeth on edge. Count to ten and realize that most of the time, they're not trying to drive you wild.

Caroline decides to talk about her daughter with her Aunt Lily over the phone. She hasn't seen her aunt in years, but they're both going to a family wedding. In fact, Caroline's daughter, Annie, who was adopted as a newborn in the United States, is now five years old. She'll be the flower girl at the wedding, and the child is really excited about it.

CAROLINE: Hey, Aunt Lily! I haven't talked to you for just about forever!

AUNT LILY: Hey yourself. My back is acting up on me, I can tell you that.

CAROLINE: Sorry to hear your back is hurting you! I hope you feel better really soon. I just wanted to let you know that my daughter Annie's going to be the flower girl at the wedding, and she's just so excited! She can't stop talking about it, she's so thrilled.

AUNT LILY: Oh, is that the little girl you adopted from somewhere, a while back? I heard about that! Better you than me, my dear! I could never be that patient, taking on another family's burden. She *is* a cute little thing, though, isn't she? Your mama sent me some pictures.

CAROLINE: Annie is no burden! She's a beautiful little girl and I thank God that she's mine. I didn't know Mom sent you some pictures, but I'm glad she did.

AUNT LILY: Yes, she's a sweet little girl. But you know, they grow up. I hope that her people weren't too, well, trashy or low-class.

CAROLINE: I would say that I am not trashy or low-class at all, Aunt Lily!

AUNT LILY: Oh for heaven's sake, I don't mean you! I mean her real mother, if you even know who she was, that woman.

CAROLINE: Annie's birth mother chose adoption to give Annie a good family—my family! She was in a difficult situation, and it was the best answer for us all, and certainly for me. I'm so happy to be Annie's mom.

AUNT LILY: But how could anyone give up their own flesh and blood, if they are normal? I mean, after all.

CAROLINE: It's not easy for a birth mother to choose adoption. It's a very hard thing to do and a brave thing, if she doesn't feel able to be a good parent herself.

AUNT LILY: I guess. What are you wearing to the wedding? A long or short dress?

Discussing Adoption with Teachers

Linda wants to tell Ms. Learned, her son's teacher, that her child, Sammy, age nine, was adopted. He's really struggling in school to get average grades, and Linda thinks it might help if Mrs. Learned knew Sammy was born in another country and didn't come to the United States until he was four years old. Here's a sample conversation.

LINDA: Hi, Ms. Learned. I wanted to get together to talk about how Sammy's doing. He's doing okay in school, isn't he?

MS. LEARNED: Yes, he's a C student, although maybe he could do better. He's a very nice boy.

LINDA: Yes. You know, it occurred to me it might be a good idea if I told you Sammy's had a lot to overcome.

MS. LEARNED: Oh, really? What's wrong? Is there a problem?

LINDA: Oh, no. It's just that we, my husband and I, adopted Sammy when he was four years old from an orphanage, where he was abandoned. Since then, he's had to learn English and adjust to a whole new culture. It was hard for him. I think he's still struggling a little.

MS. LEARNED: Oh my goodness, I had no idea! Which country? And my goodness, the child has no accent at all, I would never have known it. Maybe I should make extra allowances for Sammy after all he's been through!

LINDA: I certainly don't want you treating Sammy like some pathetic person, Ms. Learned. I just wanted you to understand a little about Sammy's background. He's come a long way from the Russian orphanage. And as for the lack of an accent, a lot of times if children learn a new language when they're little, they speak it like a native.

MS. LEARNED: My goodness, this is amazing! Wait until I tell the other teachers about this. And the children! They'll want to learn all about Russia. Sammy must know so much he could teach us all!

LINDA: Sammy isn't an expert on Russia, and his adoption is private! So please, I have to insist this information be kept confidential. We do not under any circumstances want you to tell the other teachers and certainly not the other children, unless my husband and I give you permission. This is very important to me!

MS. LEARNED: Okay, but if it's such a big secret, why did you tell me about it?

LINDA: Maybe it was a mistake, but the cat's out of the bag now. I guess I thought it might help you understand Sammy better and not push him too hard. But I don't want him seen as a pathetic person, or put on show before the other children. Adoption is only one part of Sammy. He's a great runner, he loves to draw, he struggles with reading, but is very talented musically. He's a wonderful boy with many different sides to him. Being adopted is just one aspect of Sammy.

MS. LEARNED: Well, I'll tell you a secret too. My sister was adopted and she recently passed away. I miss her something awful. She was a wonderful person, although she didn't come from Russia, like Sammy.

LINDA: I'm sorry to hear about your loss, Ms. Learned! Most adopted people are regular people who have families who love them, like you still love your sister.

Love and Honesty Are the Keys

Sometimes you may find you explain adoption awkwardly or badly or confuse your child and even yourself with what you say. This is normal. Try again at another time to express yourself, keeping in mind your underlying love for your child and your child's need for honest dialogue. Read Chapter 11 for more information on explaining adoption to your child.

Part IV

SPECIAL ISSUES

14

Coping with Medical Problems and Disabilities

WHETHER YOUR CHILD had medical problems or a disability when you adopted her or the problems developed later on, it's clearly important to help your child as much as you can, keeping in mind that if the medical problem is a serious and/or a chronic one, then you and your life partner will also need to take time off to attend to each other at regular intervals. Parenting is sometimes a 24/7 operation, but everyone deserves periodic breaks, whether they come from friends, family members, day care services, or other options.

This chapter covers medical problems that may occur directly or indirectly as the result of institutional life, such as living in an orphanage. Foster children can also be affected by institutional living because they may have lived in orphanage-like group homes or been placed with many different families, never having a chance to develop a relationship with one family. This chapter also tells how to evaluate your doctor and, if necessary, how to find a pediatrician who will help your child and work with you. Fortunately, the American Academy of Pediatrics (AAP) now acknowledges medical problems that adopted children may experience, particularly those who were adopted from other countries, and the recommendations the AAP offers to physicians are covered as well.

Effects of Institutionalization

Orphanages are bad for children, no matter how well-meaning the orphanage staff and how clean and safe the orphanage is. (And sometimes the staff is *not* so well-meaning, and neither is the institution clean or safe.) Children adopted from orphanages may suffer from many different health problems such as malnutrition, growth and developmental delays, and infectious diseases, as documented by physicians such as Christopher S. Quarles and Jeffrey H. Brodie in their 1998 article on the primary care of international adoptees in *American Family Physician*. (The article is available online at aafp.org/afp/981200ap/quarles.html.) When some institutionalized children who were subsequently adopted become school-age, they may suffer from more complex problems, such as attention deficit hyperactivity disorder (ADHD) or other emotional problems or from learning disabilities.

If you've recently (in the past six months) adopted a child from another country, you should be sure that your child is screened for diseases that are common in her native country (and may be rarely seen in the United States). The American Academy of Pediatrics recommends that a set panel of tests be done, regardless of the child's country of origin. Discuss laboratory testing with your pediatrician and make sure that your doctor follows the current recommendations of the AAP.

Many children who are adopted from orphanages will eventually "catch up" to their age peers in terms of growth and development, especially if they were adopted under the age of two or three years old, but some do not; for example, children who have fetal alcohol syndrome (FAS), a developmental delay that is caused by the heavy consumption of alcohol by the mother during pregnancy.

Being a foster child in the United States can also result in medical problems for children, and some foster children are malnourished and sickly. Because of frequent moves from home to home and the confusion that may occur with social workers requesting the forwarding of medical records, some foster children haven't received childhood injections when they should have had them.

Most parents try to obtain as much medical history information as possible about their child, but they also realize that often the information is fragmented or not available at all. Sometimes adoption agencies can obtain additional information from orphanages before the adoption or later on, and sometimes social workers can obtain more medical information from foster care files. Yet even when others make a valiant effort to obtain medical information about your child, you may still come up with no additional information. Doctors and dentists may be very disappointed by this, in our medically advanced high-technology society, but most of them will be willing to work with you.

Effects of Malnutrition

Children who have been deprived of sufficient food for long periods of time (or maybe their whole lives) may react to plentiful food in a new family by gorging on food until they vomit, by hiding and hoarding food, or by behaving in other ways that may distress their new parents. The child is acting rationally based on her old frame of reference, when she never knew when the next meal was coming. She needs time to learn that in this new family, there's always enough food and it isn't going to end.

Some families have set aside a cupboard for the malnourished child, full of nonperishable foods. The child can check the cupboard whenever she wants, and other family members aren't allowed to take her food. After a while, most children stop the constant checking for food and realize that in this family they will not be deprived of food.

Occasionally children, particularly little girls who are adopted from impoverished circumstances, may develop early puberty. Apparently the initial malnutrition, which has now been resolved, may stimulate the brain to think that it's time to turn on the hormones. As a result, it is possible for girls as young as four or five years old to begin to develop breasts and mature bodies, and to stop growing. Even subtle new signs of puberty such as underarm hair or body odor should be reported to the doctor immediately. If the child is treated early enough by an experienced endocrinologist, the doctor may be able to repress the hormones and hence the puberty. This problem was described by Raffaele Virdis and colleagues in a 1998 article in the *Archives of Disease in Childhood*.

Effects of Lack of Stimulation

The lack of stimulation that is typical of institutional settings can have an adverse effect on children's growth and development. They may suffer from psychosocial failure to thrive, language delays, sensory integration disorder, or other developmental delays. They may also suffer from attachment disorders, a topic that I cover briefly in Chapter 6.

Psychosocial Failure to Thrive

Psychosocial failure to thrive refers to children who, becasuse of emotional (psychosocial) neglect, fail to grow well despite adequate nutrition. Often there is a greater adverse effect on height than on weight, and consequently, children with psychosocial failure to thrive can sometimes appear reasonably nourished, albeit measurably shorter than average for their age.

Language Delays

Some children experience delays in mastering language because they were not engaged conversationally in an institution. They may also experience language delays for other reasons, such as neurological deficits, developmental delays, and medical or emotional problems.

Children adopted as newborns will generally be speaking in simple one-syllable words by the time they are eighteen to twenty-four months old, and will also understand many more words than they can actually speak. If you adopted your child when she was older than two or three years old from another country, you need to give your child time to master a new language as well as a completely new culture and environment. It will help if you can learn a few words in the child's native language so that you can perform basic communication.

If you think your child may have a problem with language delay, ask your pediatrician or family practitioner to help you identify a qualified professional who can perform an evaluation. Then, if a problem exists, the expert should be able to advise you how to help your child.

Keep in mind that experts have found that there is about a one-month delay for every three to four months a child has spent in an orphanage. Also, absent any evidence of organic medical problems, you can generally expect full catch-up to normal development for children adopted under the ages of two or three years old and expect significant but not necessarily full catch-up for children adopted between the ages of three and five years.

Sensory Integration Disorder and Other Developmental Delays

Some children adopted from other countries (or from the United States) may exhibit symptoms of relatively rare disorders such as sensory integration disorder. This disorder, described primarily in occupational therapy literature and not fully explored by medical doctors, is a disorder in which the child has difficulty dealing with sensory inputs, such as being touched. Some experts believe that sensory integration disorder may be a subset of autism, a long-term disorder that is often accompanied by developmental delays such as mental retardation. However, children with sensory integration disorder need not have other developmental delays, and therapy may provide considerable improvements for such children.

Sometimes a physician can identify developmental problems before the child is placed for adoption so that the adoptive parents are ready and able to deal with them. Some parents who adopt children from other countries hire American physicians to provide them with evaluations based on videotapes and medical history information that has been translated into English. However, in some cases the diagnosis cannot be made until the child has been in this country for a period of time. It's also important to know that sometimes the delay in diagnosis occurs because experts cannot identify which children will respond to early intervention developmental services.

Note: I feel strongly that anyone adopting a child from Eastern Europe should seek out the counsel of an adoption medicine physician. I specialize in adoption medicine, as do some of my colleagues nationwide. A list of adoption medicine physicians is available online at comeunity.com/adoption/health/clinics.html.

It can be devastating to learn that your child and you have such a difficult issue to contend with. Some children with fetal alcohol effects and other developmental delays can grow up to lead reasonably normal lives, while others cannot do so. It's important to work with a good pediatrician, as well as to identify and use the resources in your community and in your school system, to help you to help your child.

Effects of Abuse and Neglect

Children who have been institutionalized may have experienced physical abuse and neglect, and sometimes they've suffered from sexual abuse as well. They may also have been mistreated by staff members at the orphanage or by the older children who lived there. The longer children in orphanages or foster children have been "in the system," the greater the risk that they have suffered from abuse or neglect.

Ironically, in the United States, abuse and neglect are the key reasons why children are involuntarily taken away from their biological parents and placed into foster care. However, not all children in foster care have been abused or neglected; for example, some children are placed in foster care because their parents are unable to care for them because of health problems, psychiatric illness, incarceration, or other adverse psychosocial factors.

Children who've been abused are not used to kindness, and they may even see it as either insincere or as a precursor to abuse, because of acts of kindness in their past that preceded an assault. Children who have been sexually abused are the most difficult children to parent, according to social workers and to adoptive parents, because they may act out in sexual ways, masturbate openly, or make sexual overtures to their new parents. It's not that they are "oversexed" children, but rather that they are acting in ways that they were taught were normal. Such behaviors must be unlearned and replaced with appropriate behaviors, which can require considerable patience.

Books such as *Adoption and the Sexually Abused Child*, edited by Joan McNamara and Bernard H. McNamara (Human Services Development Institute, University of Southern Maine, 1990) and *Parenting the Hurt Child: Helping Adoptive Families Heal and Grow* by Gregory C. Keck, Ph.D., and Regina M. Kupecky, L.S.W. (Piñon Press, 2002) offer many helpful suggestions for parents whose children were abused in the past.

Early Intervention Programs for Children

If your child is age two or younger and may have some developmental delays, then consider having him or her evaluated for an early intervention

(EI) program. These are state and federally funded programs for children who need help, regardless of your family income.

Such a program may help your child so that she'll be able to perform better when she enters kindergarten. Speak with your child's pediatrician or contact your local school board or state education department for further information on early childhood intervention programs. In some states, it is the state health department that is in charge of early intervention programs. The headquarters of most states' agencies are located in the state capital.

Children under age five are entitled to a free developmental evaluation, as well as treatment services where indicated. Although EI stops at age three, local school districts are generally responsible for evaluating and providing service to children from ages three to five at no cost to parents. As with younger children, the eligibility for children ages three to five for developmental therapies depends on the extent of the child's delays. Head Start programs, in contrast, are designed to help preschool children who do not have developmental delays but are from low-income families and deemed to be at high risk for later educational and psychosocial difficulties.

If Your Child Was Disabled When You Adopted

In some cases, you may have been fully informed of your child's physical or emotional disabilities before the adoption, and you felt prepared (or you resolved to become prepared) to help your child cope with them. There are numerous types of disabilities that children may have, ranging from major to minor medical problems. Also, what may seem severe to some families doesn't loom so large to other families. For example, some families would find it very burdensome to deal with attention deficit hyperactivity disorder (ADHD), while others have an attitude that ADHD is not such a big deal, but they may think that developmental delays such as Down syndrome are too tough to cope with. Still other families might have specifically sought to adopt a child with Down syndrome, while they would regard disabilities such as blindness or deafness as too onerous for their family to handle.

Even if you knew that your child had a disability when you adopted her or him, you may not have known how difficult it would be in reality to manage the disability—or perhaps it has been easier than you anticipated. (However, most families tend to underestimate the extent of problems.) If you need help, be sure to ask others, including family members, friends, congregants in your faith group, and others. It isn't shameful to ask for help when you need it.

If Your Child Becomes Disabled After Adoption

Maybe your child was healthy at the time of the adoption, but he later developed a physical or emotional ailment. (For much more information on emotional disabilities, be sure to read Chapter 16.) Adoption agencies don't offer lifelong guarantees of health of the children they place for adoption, nor should they. You'll need to identify good doctors to help your child, and you also need a helpful network of caring friends and relatives to get you through the tough times.

Some parents report that when the child they adopted becomes disabled, their peers and family members are unsympathetic, telling them that they shouldn't have adopted a child or that they should disrupt the adoption by giving the child to the foster care system. (Even if parents wished to do this, it isn't always legally possible, depending on state laws.)

Other parents say that their friends and family stood by them and provided all the support they needed to deal with their child's serious medical problems.

Finding an Understanding Doctor

Most readers have already adopted their children, and they have also already identified a pediatrician for their children. Hopefully, your doctor is positive about adoption, and willing to learn about any medical problems that your child may have now or could experience in the future, in order to provide you with good medical advice.

If you adopted your child from another country, your doctor may not be very knowledgeable about illnesses that children in Asia, South America, countries in the former Soviet Union, or other countries may have, such as parasitic infections and diseases such as tuberculosis, hepatitis, and others. But if he or she is willing to listen and learn, that's a very positive indicator that you're working with the right doctor for your child.

Evaluating Your Current Doctor

How do you know, other than by your general observations of your doctor, if he or she is the right physician for your child? One way is to ask yourself the following questions with regard to the interactions that you've had so far with the doctor:

- Has your doctor clearly explained every diagnosis and what you're expected to do about it as a parent?
- Is your doctor available if your child has an emergency, or does the doctor have a backup physician you can call?
- Does your doctor seem to like your child and children in general?
- When you ask questions, does the doctor give clear responses?
- If the doctor seems unsure how to treat a medical problem, is he willing to do further research and/or contact other physicians with more expertise?

If you answer no to any of the above questions, you may wish to consider locating another physician for your child. If you answer no to more than two questions, you should get another doctor for your child.

Identifying a New Doctor

If you need to identify a new physician for your child, find out if your insurance company has a list of approved doctors. Often the health insurance company has investigated the physicians on its list, excluding anyone with any serious history of major malpractice claims. However, being on an insurance company's list of approved doctors doesn't necessarily guarantee good quality of care. In addition, sometimes doctors who are not on the insurance company's list might be better for your child, and worth paying an extra "out-of-network" fee.

Other good ways to find a new pediatrician or family practitioner include asking your friends and any family members living in the area if they can recommend a good doctor to you. In addition, often other practitioners can offer recommendations, such as your own primary care physician, as well as any other doctors you see. You may also wish to ask your dentist and your pharmacist if they're aware of good pediatricians in your area.

Talk to parents in local adoption groups in your community to gain recommendations for pediatricians. Also, if you live near a teaching hospital (preferably a children's hospital), look to this source for your doctor. These physicians are generally knowledgeable and well qualified.

Interviewing the Doctor

When you think you have a good candidate to provide medical care for your child, be sure to interview her first before signing up. Do so even when you have to pay a fee to see the doctor. It's also better to choose your doctor in a calm period, whenever possible, than when your child is in the midst of a medical crisis.

As you talk to the doctor, ask yourself if you feel comfortable with her. Can she look you in the eyes? Does she explain medical problems in everyday language, apart from medical jargon? If so, these are important points in the doctor's favor.

Be sure to check out the waiting room and the staff while you are there. Don't expect a perfectly orderly waiting room, because children do scatter toys. But is it basically clean and safe-looking? As for the staff, do they seem calm and organized, as well as friendly and caring? These are also pluses, because the staff is your link to the doctor. Even an excellent doctor needs good staff as a backup.

15

Children Adopted in Transracial and International Adoptions

IF YOU ADOPT a child who's of another race or ethnicity than yours, adoption professionals and others will usually refer to this adoption as a transracial adoption. If you adopt a biracial child born to parents of different races, such as black and white, this is also considered a transracial adoption. Many people don't realize it, but transracial adoptions also include adopting a child of another race or ethnicity from another country; for example, if your child was born in China and you are not Asian, this is a transracial adoption as well as an international adoption.

Transracial adoptions are usually very successful for both the parents and the children when the child was adopted as an infant or toddler. International adoptions of young children are also usually successful.

Children adopted as older children can present greater problems for their families and themselves, generally not because of their race or ethnicity, but more often because of the abuse, neglect, and rejection that they often have experienced before you adopted them. This is also the case for same-race, same-country adoptions as well as for transracial and international adoptions.

Sometimes the racism that children experience in this country makes a child's life difficult, and parents who think that love will smooth over all problems aren't being realistic. Love helps, of course, but for a nonwhite child, it doesn't take away the pain of hearing a racial slur or seeing the shock on the faces of people when his or her white parents walk into a school function.

Interestingly, negative racial comments may come more often from people of your own race rather than of the race of your child. If you are white and adopt a black child, it's unlikely that blacks will make cruel or demeaning remarks to you and your child, but some white people may do so. Families who've adopted transracially often report that black families are very supportive of them. Some organizations, however, such as the National Association of Black Social Workers, have been openly opposed to transracial adoption.

It's also true that nonadoptive parents often face difficult problems with racism; for example, Diana's father was a blue-eyed white man and her mother was from the Philippines. Diana married a white man and they had a child, a blue-eyed, blonde-haired daughter. When Diana goes out with her child, even to the supermarket, people frequently tell her that her child looks nothing like her. This is painful for Diana, and she's struggling to come up with what, if anything, to tell total strangers about her racial heritage. Diana thinks it's likely people who don't say anything believe her daughter was adopted, which may be preferable to saying she couldn't possibly be her child's "real mother."

This chapter talks about transracial adoption, including a discussion of the comprehensive and long-term studies performed by Rita Simon and Howard Altstein. In addition, it addresses issues with transracial adoption or international adoption that may arise as your child grows up. For example, many studies have shown that some adolescents who are adopted transracially have a difficult time. Not only do they receive teasing and bullying from children their own age, but they are also struggling with the identity conflicts that characterize adolescence for most teenagers.

Some studies, such as those by Simon and Altstein, have shown that young adults who struggled as adolescents have a much better relationship with their parents when they are young adults. Of course, you're not "there" yet, because you're still parenting children younger than adults, so I'll talk about parenting issues that may concern you right now.

The Challenges of Transracial Adoptions

When you adopt a child of another race, it changes how others regard you and your other family members. Of course your own race hasn't changed at all, but the race of one family member affects all family members. In fact, if you adopt a child who was born to one black parent and one white parent, many people would consider your family to now be a black family. Strangely, the same doesn't appear true if you adopt an Asian child. You usually aren't perceived to have become an Asian family when you adopt a Chinese child or to be transformed into a Hispanic family if you adopt a child from Guatemala.

Based on research and comments from families who have adopted transracially, the challenge is to offer your children opportunities where they can meet other people of the same race or ethnicity. If the child was born in another culture, she may enjoy the opportunity to learn about the foods and traditions of the land. At the same time, some parents run the risk of overcompensating, and their children report that they're sick of going to culture camps to learn about other lands, they don't care if they forget their native Spanish, and they just want to be like everyone else. Sometimes striking a good balance can be difficult for parents.

Your timing also needs to be right. Some parents have reported taking their newly adopted Korean child to a function celebrating Korean culture, and the child was terrified. They realized that the child mistakenly believed that the parents were trying to reindoctrinate her into Korean culture because they were planning to send her back to Korea. They quickly assured the child that she was their "forever" child, and they had only gone to the Korean party for fun. The parents stayed away from Korean functions for several years until they were sure their child felt secure.

Studies of Children Adopted in Transracial/Transethnic Adoptions

Studies on children who have been adopted by parents of other races have shown many positive results. And yet organizations such as the National

Association of Black Social Workers have been fervently opposed to transracial adoptions since the 1970s, and likened such adoptions to "racial genocide." Some social workers continue to believe that it's better for a black child to remain in foster care than to be adopted by a white family. (Ironically, many foster parents are white.) Many experts believe that whites are still discriminated against in adoption, despite several different laws that ban race as a consideration in the adoption of children.

Rita Simon and Howard Altstein began studying adoptive families and their transracially adopted children in 1971, and they revisited many of their subjects again in 1979, 1984, and 1991, obtaining a wealth of data. The adopted children were black, white, Korean, and several were Native Americans. Many of the children that Simon and Altstein have studied were young adults in 1991.

The researchers were able to interview parents, adopted children, and their nonadopted siblings. Most of the children were adopted when they were under the age of one year. Simon and Altstein's study results, as well as the findings of many other researchers, are summarized in the book *Adoption Across Borders: Serving the Children in Transracial and Intercountry Adoptions* (Rowman and Littlefield Publishers, 2000).

According to Simon and Altstein, their key finding in 1972 was that nonwhite adopted children and their nonadopted siblings did not show any preference to white dolls over black dolls. (At the time this was significant, because black social workers feared that black adopted children would invariably choose a white doll over a black one, which might indicate children thought whites were better than blacks.) Said the researchers, "It [the white doll] was not considered smarter, prettier, nicer, and so forth, than the black doll by either the white or black children." At the same time, the children accurately identified their own race, despite fears of some experts that children who were adopted by parents of a different race would have racial confusion.

In 1984, most of the children studied by Simon and Altstein were adolescents, and the researchers found that many parents had introduced elements of other cultures into their lives; for example, the parents of black children attended black churches and had sought out black children as friends for their children while the parents of Korean or Native American children had located music and books on the native culture, as well as tried out recipes and gone to local ethnic events. Interestingly, the children were the ones who began to back away from the black or ethnic activities, telling their parents such things as "Not every dinner conversation has to be a lesson in black history," or "We are more interested in basketball and football than in ceremonial dances."

The researchers tested the self-esteem levels of the adopted and non-adopted children and found that there was virtually no difference among them.

In 1991 the researchers visited as many of their subjects as they could for the last time. The follow-up sample was comprised of forty-one black children, fourteen children of other races than the adoptive parents (most were Korean-born), and thirteen white adoptees. There were also thirty children born to the adoptive families.

The researchers asked the adoptive parents, "Thinking back, and with the knowledge of hindsight and the experiences you have accumulated, would you have done what you did—adopt a child of a different race?" The responses: 92 percent said yes, 4 percent said they weren't sure, and 4 percent said no. Among those who said no (three people), two said that the child had physical and emotional problems that were very difficult to deal with, and race wasn't the problem. The other family just said it wasn't a successful experience.

The transracially adopted children (now adults) were also asked how they thought the fact that they had a different racial background from their brothers and sisters who were born to the family affected their relationships with them as they grew up. Nearly 90 percent said it didn't matter, while the rest were split between whether there was a positive effect, negative effect, or they weren't sure what the effect was.

The researchers also asked the adopted adults who they would turn to if they had a serious problem. The transracially adopted adults were as likely or more likely to turn to their parents or siblings than the white adoptees or the nonadopted children in their family.

Coping with Questions as Children Grow

Even when children are only three or four years old, they may notice their skin color is different from yours or their hair texture is not the same. If you have curly hair, your small child will want to have curly hair too, just like yours. This is understandable, because your child loves you and wants to resemble you. However, if you're white, it can be painful to hear your young child ask you to "wash out" his skin color, thinking if you scrub him hard enough, his skin color will match yours. It's important for children to understand they are beautiful as they are.

Many families take an active role in seeking out other families who are the same race as their adopted child. In their book *Inside Transracial Adoption*, authors Gail Steinberg and Beth Hall offer numerous practical suggestions for parents who've adopted children of a different race than their own, including attending meetings by people of other races. However, they caution that you should approach the issue with sensitivity.

For example, let's say you adopted a child from Korea and wish to meet Korean adults and children. According to Steinberg and Hall, it's best to seek a group that is open and receptive to you. Thus, "approaching a Korean church that is the only Korean language church of its kind in the state may be more difficult than approaching a Korean community center which has a fully bilingual program. The church is probably working to maintain its primary culture, making it less open to outsiders [like you] who may tend to 'dilute' the effort, than the community center which is obviously trying to bridge the issues for Korean-Americans in living biculturally."

Some white parents have reported that after they adopted African-American children, they moved to mixed neighborhoods that included both black and white families. Others stayed in the same neighborhood but changed their church membership to a church with both black and white members or made other arrangements to interact with black children and adults.

Occasionally, moving a family to a mixed neighborhood doesn't work out well, despite the best of intentions. In one case described in *Adoption Across Borders: Serving the Children in Transracial and Intercountry Adoptions*, a parent who had adopted black children moved his family to a less affluent and mixed race neighborhood. He became horrified to discover that his children had begun to perceive blacks as people who take drugs and get into trouble—because that was a common behavior in the new neighborhood. Realizing this, the parents moved the family away from the neighborhood. In this unusual situation, parents should explain that most blacks are good people and that the problem in the old neighborhood was hopelessness and poverty, and not race.

Some parents have chosen to take their children for a tour of their birth country to help them gain a firsthand experience of their cultural heritage, although most experts recommend such a trip be delayed for at least a few years after the adoption (in case the child may fear she's being returned to where she was born, despite what her parents tell her to the contrary).

Preschool Children

In general, most preschoolers are pleased to accept whatever explanation their adoptive parents offer to explain why their skin color, eyes, or other features aren't just like those of their adoptive parents. However, even preschoolers are sometimes subjected to cruel comments from others. For example, Lori's brother asked her when she was going to have her Chinese daughter's eyes "fixed" with plastic surgery. Lori controlled her temper and told her brother that there was nothing wrong with Luci's eyes, and they didn't *need* to be fixed.

Unfortunately, four-year-old Luci heard the comments, and she wondered aloud to Lori, why did Uncle Jimmy think that her eyes were bad? And was Mommy sure that her eyes were really okay and didn't need to be fixed? This was both a problem and an opportunity for Lori, who decided to concentrate on the opportunity aspect in very simply explaining racial differences to Luci. She told Luci that God made people in different beautiful ways, but sometimes other people forgot this or were somehow confused by it, and that's very sad.

School-Age Children

Because what peers think about them becomes increasingly important to school-age children, it can be difficult or even embarrassing to them to have a parent who doesn't resemble them racially. Children want to be like everyone else, and they don't want to stand out in a crowd, especially because of how their mother or father looks in comparison to them.

School-age children may also wonder who they should gravitate toward at school, if there is a racial mixture of children in their school. (If possible, parents should try to seek out schools where there are children of different races so that, for example, your Chinese daughter doesn't feel odd because no one else in the school is Asian.) Many transracially adopted children tend to gravitate toward the race of their adoptive parents, and many also date and marry individuals of their adoptive parents' race.

Adolescents and Racial Issues

Probably the hardest time for adopted children whose parents are not of the same race or ethnicity is during adolescence, when pretty much everything is harder—or at least, it seems that way to the adolescent. Children may resent their parents for adopting them out of their race and fervently wish, aloud and to themselves, that they'd never been adopted. In their long-term studies of transracially adopted children, Simon and Altstein found that attitudes toward their parents improved once the children had moved on from adolescence to adulthood. This finding would probably be true for same-race adopted children or nonadopted children.

Adolescence is a time of teasing from peers as well as general anxiety about oneself and one's appearance. Parents can be sympathetic, but they can't take all the sting out of being an adolescent. What you can do is listen to your teenager and be as supportive as possible.

Dealing with Racism

It would be great if everyone valued each other as individuals with unique talents and abilities. Sadly, racism still happens, with name-calling from children and adults. Yes, adults should know better, but sometimes they don't, and they teach their bigoted attitudes to their children.

Although they may think they're color-blind, even parents find that they notice their child's skin color. Peggy Soule, an adoptive parent, described it this way in *The Adoption Option Complete Handbook 2000–2001* (Prima Publishing, 1999): "As a white mother who adopted an African-American infant, I was sure I would not be aware of his color. How wrong I was. His beautiful skin is part of who he is, and I see it clearly every time

I hug him—even today at thirty years of age. It is also what the police see when he is driving a car."

It's not wrong for parents to see their children's skin color. But as Soule points out, others didn't see her son's skin color as beautiful, and instead sometimes he was perceived as a potential problem, merely because of his skin color and nothing else.

Racism can make a normally calm and pleasant person feel a blind rage. How dare anyone say such a terrible thing to your child? It's bad enough when people insult you directly, but when they take aim at your child, that really hurts. Sometimes you must force yourself to walk away, when a confrontation might lead to violence and could frighten your child even more than she already is. You don't have to ever agree with what racist people say, but you can't beat those bad ideas out of them.

Often racism is far more subtle than an uneducated person making a direct racial slur; for example, some parents complain of racism in the schools, where it's assumed because their children are black, biracial, or of another nonwhite race, that they need to be in special classes for slow learners.

Before you spring to your child's defense, investigate whether your child's real problem may be that he needs some extra help because of a learning disability or other problem with academic achievement. After reviewing the evidence, if the underlying problem is racism, you'll need to defend your child against it. Referring to studies on transracial adoption; the long-term studies by Simon and Altstein, authors of *Adoption Across Borders: Serving the Children in Transracial and Intercountry Adoptions*, as well as other studies, may help you because they show that most transracial adoptions are successful.

Talking about Biracial Issues

What if your child's biological heritage is not of one but of two or more races? Perhaps your child's birth mother was black and her birth father was Caucasian. With which group should the child most identify with and relate to, black or white?

Some children of different races are challenging such views. For example, the famed golfer Tiger Woods has said that he is "Caublasian," a word he made up to reflect the fact that his parents are of white, black, and Asian racial backgrounds.

It can be confusing for the biracial child to fashion her own identity, which is further complicated by whether others primarily identify her as black, white, Asian, or another race. Who does she sit with in the cafeteria at school, the white kids or the black kids? It's an unfortunate reality that often kids congregate along racial lines.

Parents need to help the child understand who she is by talking to the child and welcoming questions she may have, as well as telling her that sometimes people will make cruel remarks, sometimes on purpose and sometimes unthinkingly.

General Parenting Advice

It's not possible in one chapter to describe everything that you can do to help your child adopted transracially from the United States or from another country. But here's some general advice, which has helped others.

1. Associate with adults and children of the same race as your child. This may mean joining a faith group or club with members who are of different races. Even if you have to drive a long while to get there, realize that it's important to your child. Drive there.

2. Consider culture camps as a summertime activity for school-age or adolescent children adopted from Korea, India, and other countries. These are opportunities for children to meet other children, often adopted from the same country as they were. Ask for information about the camp first and read the brochure about it. (Culture camps advertise in such publications as *Adoptive Families*.) There may also be some information about the camp on a website on the Internet. Ask for the names of other parents whose children have previously attended and talk to them about their child's experience.

    Keep in mind that the first time your child goes to a culture camp or any camp, she may be very apprehensive, but if you've checked it out and it looks like a good opportunity, you may wish to encourage her to go anyway. However, don't force your child to go to a culture camp year after year if she's no longer interested.

3. Understand sometimes people in other racial groups may perceive *you* as the outsider. Make sure it's okay and that you would be at least tolerated if you attended cultural events meant for Asian, Latino, or other groups. Call up and ask the leaders of the event if some people who attend are white or black or whatever race you are. (Don't simply ask them if it's okay to go, because by asking the question that way, you put them in a racist box if they say no.)

4. Realize sometimes strangers or even people you know will make racist remarks, and it'll hurt your child. Find ways to cope with such incidents. Authors Hall and Steinberg say some families develop code words, such as "bubbles" or "Spike," which they use when people are bothering them in public and they're getting upset. One family member says, "It's bubbling outside," or "Spike needs me," or some similar phrase that signals to other family members, "It's time to get out of here as soon as possible."

5. Realize you can't transform all racists. If you encounter racism in people who are important in your child's life, such as family members, you need to call them on it, telling them you will not accept such remarks or such behaviors. In most cases, they'll back down. If they don't, you'll need to limit contact with them.

6. Don't see racism everywhere. Sometimes people make innocent or stupid remarks and they really don't mean anything by it. However, read my next point.

7. Don't blow off complaints from your child about racist remarks others make to him or her. If your child's upset, it's not enough to tell him or her merely that someone really didn't "mean it." Maybe not, but racist remarks still hurt. Sympathize and empathize, and know your child must learn to cope with these difficult situations, with your help.

8. Realize that if you have other children who aren't members of a racial minority, sometimes they'll receive verbal abuse about their sibling, particularly from peers. It's hard to know who to be loyal to sometimes, your annoying brother or your friend? Parents need to make it clear

that, in most cases, loyalty to your family comes first, and this is their sister or brother that others are talking about, not some stereotype.

9. Pay attention to your child's responses to your attempts at cultural education. If you're overdoing the international recipes or talking too much about the child's country of origin or black heritage, your child will usually tell you or at least show you in his body language. Provide opportunities to learn about food, music, art, and other cultural choices, but don't make it a cultural force-feeding.

10. Don't overreact. If your child says he'd rather go to a white child's party than go to a black church, this doesn't mean your child is a racist. Maybe he likes parties better than going to church. However, if you think your child is demeaning his race or that of a sibling, address it. Tell him about famous people of the same race or about contributions that people of his race have made. (The famous people don't have to be adopted people.) If you don't know of any such people, then do some research and find some! In addition, whenever possible, talk about people of the same race as your child in your community whom you admire, such as a clergyperson, teacher, judge, and so forth.

It's not possible to cover every scenario that may occur to you and your child adopted transracially and/or from another country. The key is to keep your eyes and ears open, and listen to your child. Provide opportunities to meet and interact with other people of her race or ethnicity, but don't force them. Realize that sometimes your child may feel sad about being adopted and race may or may not be a part of that sadness. And know that studies indicate that most children who were adopted transracially or in international adoptions are well-adjusted and happy.

16

If Your Child Has Emotional Problems

MOST ADOPTED CHILDREN are emotionally healthy individuals who grow up to be normal adults. Many clinical studies have shown this to be true, although some therapists emphasize a few studies in which some adopted children or adults have demonstrated serious emotional problems. Often studies lump together individuals adopted as older children who had been abused with children adopted as babies. They all were "adopted," so to some researchers, they're all the same. However, common sense indicates that the majority of adopted children and adults are functioning well in society.

There are about 1.5 million adopted children living in the United States, according to U.S. Census Bureau statistics released in 2003, and this number doesn't include adopted adults. If most were severely emotionally disturbed, harming themselves or others or engaging in criminal acts, that would be a story the media couldn't resist. You haven't heard or read such a story because there isn't one.

At the same time, it's undeniable that some adopted children do experience moderate to severe emotional problems as they grow up, and if your child experiences such problems, she needs your help.

This chapter describes how to tell when your child is having problems that indicate he needs professional therapy, as well as how to find a good therapist. It also covers how to deal with your distressing emotions generated by your child's emotional problems. In addition, if you're married or in a serious relationship, your partner will be affected by your child's emotional problems, and the chapter addresses this as well.

A Note About Adoption Studies

You may be curious about studies on adopted children and their emotional health, so I'll mention a few here. But keep in mind, the key issue for you to consider is if *your* child has a problem, regardless of what's going on with other children.

Adoption studies generally compare something about adopted individuals to people who weren't adopted. Many adoption studies use data from Sweden or Denmark, because these countries maintain a great deal of data on adopted children and their biological parents, and some data on adoptive parents. It's unclear if Scandinavian adoption studies can be generalized to American adoptees, because there are many cultural, racial, and ethnic differences between Scandinavians and Americans.

This is an important issue because in 1994, the Search Institute in Minnesota released the results of a large study examining the outcomes for 881 adolescents adopted as infants and toddlers by families in the Midwest. By adolescence, the children were as well-adjusted as nonadopted children, and in a few areas, such as knowing they were loved and identifying with their parents, they scored higher than kids born to their families. More recently in 2003, the preliminary results from an ongoing study at the University of Minnesota, the Sibling Interaction and Behavior Study (SIBS), indicate that in terms of mental health, adopted siblings are little different from nonadopted siblings.

In contrast, a study in the medical journal *Lancet* in 2002 indicated that a significant number of children in Sweden adopted from other countries experienced very serious behavioral and emotional problems when compared to nonadopted children in Sweden. Another study, published in a 2001 issue of the *Journal of Abnormal Child Psychology*, which used reports of parents (rather than diagnoses from mental health professionals), found that adopted children had a higher incidence of symptoms of attention deficit disorder and oppositional defiant disorder than nonadopted children. Very important to keep in mind is one finding of this study. According to the authors, "the clearest associated risk factors include histories of pre-adoption abuse/neglect, later age of adoption, prenatal drug exposure, and placement in multiple foster homes prior to adoption."

There are many other studies indicating problems with adopted children, with other studies that come to the exact opposite conclusion.

Before knowing if a study might be useful, you need to check how old the children in the study were when adopted and if they had identifiable emotional problems prior to the adoption, among other factors.

To take one example of a study of problems with adopted children, consider a journal article that Marshall Schecter, a psychiatrist, wrote in 1960 in the *Archives of General Psychiatry*. It has been repeatedly used to supposedly prove adopted children are more disturbed than nonadopted children. Dr. Schecter had 16 adopted patients of 120 patients.

Let's take a brief look at some of his adopted patients. According to the article, three of the children were over age nine when they were adopted. In addition, some had been under extreme stress; for example, in one case, a pediatrician told the new adoptive parents their child, age fourteen months, must be immediately toilet trained as a top priority. Schecter reported toilet training "seemed to become the condition for acceptance into this family."

So, the question becomes, in Schecter's patients, was it being adopted that caused the children's psychiatric problems, or was it problems they faced before adoption—or maybe unrealistic expectations imposed on the children after the adoption (as with the toddler who was supposed to immediately master toilet training)?

Considering many different studies performed on adopted individuals, it's impossible to single out one study and say, this is it, *this* study definitively proves adopted children are emotionally sicker *or* they are as healthy as nonadopted children.

Studies have shown, however, that emotional and behavior problems are more common among children who are adopted as older children, as well as those who have lived in multiple foster homes, who have been abused or neglected, or who were born to drug or alcohol-abusing parents. Despite this, even children falling into these categories don't necessarily experience emotional problems. All we can say for sure is that some adopted children have emotional problems, and if *your child* needs help, it's your job as a parent to seek help.

Know the Therapist's Views on Adoption

If you need to consult with a mental health professional to help your child, it's important to select the right therapist. One problem with some therapists is that they "clinicalize" adoption. In my opinion, too many are too quick to focus on adoption as the sole or main cause of any problems. Such a therapist can be more damaging than no therapist at all.

Of course, your child's emotional problems *could* stem from an adoption-related conflict, such as an identity issue, confusion about her past, or something else somehow tied in with adoption. But to help your child (if a therapist is needed), find a therapist who doesn't see adoption itself as a negative and who understands that a child's problem may be something else altogether or may be caused by a combination of factors.

Therapists also shouldn't assume an adoption issue is *never* a problem, because sometimes it is. Often it's not being adopted so much as something that happened before the adoption or mistaken ideas a child may have, whether the erroneous ideas are about adoption in general or his adoption in particular. Although it's less likely you'll find a therapist who assumes adoption is never a problem, it happens. A therapist should consider adoption as one possible piece of the puzzle of what's troubling your child.

Consider That There May Be a Problem

Just figuring out whether your child *has* a problem can be difficult. For example, it's easy to deny your child may have a serious emotional problem, because few people want to admit to themselves that their child may be emotionally ill. It's very painful to think something's wrong with your child. On the other hand, don't leap to the conclusion that because your child was adopted and is, for example, acting like a surly teenager, this automatically means you must rush her to the nearest therapist. It doesn't.

Because you love your child and you're close to her, it can be hard to determine if the child needs a therapist. Sometimes it's obvious, as when a child has harmed herself or others or is clearly on a destructive path, and it's evident that therapy is needed. Any child who seems suicidal or severely violent needs therapy. If, however, you take a child to a therapist soon after you've adopted her, make sure the therapist understands that at least part of the conflict may be the child's struggles to adapt to her new environment.

Other times, it's not clear an emotional problem exists. You don't want to overreact and force therapy on a child who doesn't need it. Discuss the existence of a possible problem with your child and your life partner.

Don't forget about your pediatrician or family practitioner—she can also offer valuable advice. Your doctor can assess the child or refer you to someone else to assess him.

The *timing* of your child's distressing behavior is important. If you just adopted siblings from Russia, and their behavior on the plane ride home was horrible, and you think maybe the kids are emotionally disturbed, think how hard it was for them to leave their culture to go on a long plane ride with people they don't know. Orphanages are awful, but kids get used to them. And they'll nearly always get used to you and grow to love you. But the transition period may last weeks or months as the children adjust to your lifestyle. This is also true if you adopt a child from foster care.

Differentiating Normal Behavior from Problem Behavior

Children can act strange sometimes, and a lot of bizarre or silly behavior can fall within the normal range. So how do you know if your child's behavior is a problem and he may urgently need help? Some indicators of a need for therapy are as follows:

1. A child who constantly talks about death or says that he or she wishes to die. (This child needs therapy right away. Children can and do commit suicide.)
2. A child's grades are much lower than in the past, and teachers are complaining about the grades and/or behavior. (This may indicate an emotional problem or could mean your child has a learning disability, attention deficit hyperactivity disorder, or other problem.)
3. Your child has gained or lost a noticeable amount of weight, with no corresponding growth spurt in the case of weight gain. (Weight

changes may also mean a child has a medical problem, so bring it up with your pediatrician.)

4. Nothing seems to make your child happy, and he or she has lost interest in previously enjoyed activities.
5. The child has trouble getting to sleep or staying asleep almost every night.
6. Your child has complained that people are after her or trying to harm her in some vague way or a way that sounds ludicrous to you.
7. Your school-age child frequently talks to herself or seems to be talking to someone else when there's no one there.
8. The child is constantly performing the same ritual over and over. The child also seems obsessed with counting meaningless things.
9. Your child is exhibiting self-harming behavior, such as cutting or scratching herself. (This child may be suicidal and needs therapy urgently.)

If your child has exhibited any behaviors described in these nine statements, he or she may have an emotional problem. Some possible emotional problems are described in the following sections, although there are many different emotional problems children can experience.

Maybe It's Depression

Depression is a very common problem, and it's highly treatable. If several of the examples of behaviors described in statements 1 through 5 seem to fit your child, particularly being obsessed with death, it's likely your child has a problem with depression. If so, your child needs to see a therapist. Clinical depression is more than feeling sad for a day or so and then bouncing back to normal again. Instead, clinical depression is a severely depressed mood over time, and it requires treatment that is provided by a mental health professional.

The good news about depression is that with medication and psychotherapy, most depressed children and adolescents will improve. But without treatment, some children will become much sicker. Some children, even preadolescents, will commit suicide if they're depressed enough. It can be difficult for a parent to gauge the depth of depression, so if there's any suicide talk at all, immediately take your child to the pediatrician or a mental health professional to be evaluated. Even if your child isn't suicidal, it's bad parenting to allow a depressed child to continue without getting needed help.

Some children (both adopted and nonadopted) go through phases when they may wear only black clothing and heavy makeup (even boys) or may dye their hair strange colors. It's up to you, as a parent, to try to determine whether it's a fashion statement or possible depression. If your child isn't obsessed with death and is doing okay in school, it could be the clothes or image that appeals to her.

Other Possible Problems

If your child says others are trying to harm her, as in statement 6, she may be right. Sometimes children do torment other children. Being bullied is not a normal part of childhood that should be tolerated. (Some teasing is normal, however.) A bully instills fear in his victims and may try to make them act against their will. A bully *wants* to distress victims. In contrast, people who tease may not realize they are upsetting anyone.

Your child also may be exhibiting paranoid behavior. (This is very rare.) If your child hears voices in her head and carries on conversations with herself, this may indicate a mental disorder such as schizophrenia, in which a person has trouble telling reality from what's imaginary. Of course, many children playact or exhibit behavior more appropriate for younger children. The key is if the child can distinguish reality from what is pretend.

If the child is constantly performing meaningless rituals associated with counting things, as in statement 8, she may have a problem with obsessive-compulsive disorder (OCD). This is also possible if the child is very worried about germs and constantly washing her hands, although excessive hand-washing is not the only form of obsessive behavior.

The ninth statement covers children who self-mutilate, which can be very dangerous and terribly frightening to parents. This is unusual behavior, and a child who acts in this manner is deeply distressed and needs help from a physician and a mental health professional. She may be suffering from depression or another emotional illness.

Questions to Ask Yourself

The questions listed earlier on children's behaviors can't cover all emotional problems, so it's a good idea to ask yourself general questions about your child to determine if he or she may need a therapist. Consider the following questions in relation to your child.

- Based on how long your child has been in your family, is his behavior deteriorating? (Factor in the impact of adolescence, which can be difficult.) Did you adopt the child a few months ago or a few years ago? A recently adopted child (unless a baby) may exhibit emotional difficulties because he's adjusting. But if a child's behavior is spiraling downward after years in your family, therapy is often a good idea.

- Is your child exhibiting behavior dangerous to himself and/or others? Wanting to drive a motorcycle doesn't count. Stealing a motorcycle and driving it while drunk are behaviors that signify a problem.

- Realistically, what might happen if you *don't* take your child to a therapist? If you think your child will stay about the same, and the behaviors, although annoying, seem in the normal range, therapy may not be indicated. Conversely, if you think your child seems to be getting worse, your child may need therapy. If you think your child may burn your house down, the child needs therapy. For most people, their child will be between these two extremes. If so, ask yourself which extreme your child is closer to—the okay child or the disturbed child? If it's the disturbed child, find a therapist.

- Are you resisting therapy for your child because you think the neighbors, your boss, family members, or others might find out? Maybe you think this revelation would make you look like a failure or cause your child to be stigmatized. If so, get over it. Sometimes parents must take actions that are painful and embarrassing.

- Are you considering therapy because someone in your family or a teacher thinks your child needs it, even though you think your child is fine? Maybe they're right. But maybe not. You're the one who should make that call.

- Last, what does your "gut" tell you? Even if everything points to *not* taking your child to a therapist, but somehow the situation feels wrong to you, consider your basic instincts. Sometimes they're valid.

Finding a Competent and Caring Therapist

It can be a challenge to find a good therapist unbiased about adoption, either pro or con. In fact, it's better to work with a therapist who doesn't purport to know anything about adoption, but who's open to learning how it *might* be affecting the child.

Therapists who identify themselves as "adoption therapists" are more likely to find adoption as the cause behind every problem than therapists who don't use "adoption" in their title or advertisements. The same situation would be true if you took your child to a therapist who specialized in attention deficit disorder: the probability is high she'd find your child's main problem was attention deficit disorder. People generally find what they're looking for, even when they're therapists.

Sorting Them Out: Psychiatrists, Psychologists, and Social Workers

A psychiatrist is a medical doctor who specializes in emotional problems, and can prescribe medications. Most psychiatrists who prescribe drugs rely upon antidepressants or antianxiety drugs, as well as medications for attention deficit disorder and other emotional problems. On rare occasions, if the child is severely disturbed and has lost touch with the real world, the doctor may prescribe an antipsychotic drug.

Some psychiatrists provide "talk therapy" (such as cognitive-behavioral therapy) where problems are discussed, and the child is trained to challenge irrational ideas, such as "Everyone should like me, and if everyone doesn't like me, that means I'm bad." If a child needs to talk things through and a psychiatrist doesn't provide this service, she'll often recommend a therapist.

A psychologist is not a doctor, and cannot prescribe medications. Most psychologists have doctorates (Ph.D.s) in clinical psychology or counseling. Psychologists rely on talking with patients to help them resolve problems. In very young children, play therapy or behavioral therapy may be used instead of talk therapy.

Some therapists are social workers. Social workers usually have a master's degree in social work (M.S.W.). A social worker usually concentrates on identifying problems and then seeking practical solutions, and social workers also provide therapy. Social workers can't prescribe medications.

Identifying a Therapist to Help Your Child

The worst way to find a therapist is to look in the yellow pages of your telephone directory and pick Dr. Adams because she's the first child psychiatrist listed. And don't select Dr. Jones because he has a huge ad purporting to be the best psychiatrist (or psychologist) for troubled children. Either therapist might be fine or could be disastrous. You need to make some further inquiries.

Ask other people you know for recommendations. Yes, they may question you about what's wrong with your child (or you). Keep your answers to a minimum, saying, for example, your child is having some "problems" and you'd like to consult with someone who might help. If your child's physician asks for details, it's okay to provide them, because she's supposed to maintain confidentiality. If your neighbor or your aunt asks for details, limit them, because the whole family may quickly be alerted, and may recall it for years, well after the problem may be completely resolved.

Should you ask your child's teacher for help in recommending a therapist? I advise against it. Although it's important to obtain information on problems a child is experiencing in school, I think it's best to obtain therapy recommendations elsewhere. Often, the teacher may simply refer you to a therapist she knows another parent is taking a child to, and may have no knowledge of the therapist herself. Also, the teacher should not be personally invested in the choice of the therapist.

Consider taking the following steps in finding a therapist for your child:

1. Ask the child's pediatrician for recommendations.
2. If the child has other physicians, ask them for recommendations for a therapist.
3. Call the local mental health association and ask for names of therapists who treat children with a range of emotional disorders.
4. If you live near a large university with a medical school, call the university's psychiatry department to obtain a referral.
5. Ask close friends and also consider asking relatives for their recommendations.
6. Some national organizations may be able to help you identify a therapist; for example, Children and Adults with Attention Deficit Disorder (CHADD) is a national organization with state chapters for parents. Contact this organization through its website, chadd.org.

Interviewing a Therapist

Before you decide to work with a particular therapist, you and your child should meet the therapist in person. A telephone screening may provide a few details, but can't replace a face-to-face meeting. When you meet the therapist, note not only how you feel about him but also how your child is reacting to the therapist. You may also wish to meet the therapist without your child being present, so you can form your own evaluation. If the therapist doesn't share your values or seems somehow wrong, you may not wish your child to meet him.

Don't hire a therapist until your child meets her too. If you think a therapist is wonderful but your child dislikes her, despite several interactions, don't make a commitment. Your child may be behaving irrationally, but there also may be something about the therapist that feels wrong to her. If so, your child won't cooperate, and you'll waste time and money, as well as potentially squander your child's emotional health. So keep looking.

Should you tell a therapist your child was adopted in the first meeting? I would. A good therapist will ask how old the child was when the adoption occurred, what were the circumstances of the adoption, what pre-adoption information (if any) was available, and whether you have any information on the birth parents.

These sorts of factual questions are good questions to ask. However, if a therapist assumes a blaming or ignoring attitude toward you not apparent before the therapist heard about the adoption, this relationship probably won't work. Even if a therapist behaves favorably and professionally toward your child, if you are the presumed cause of the problem (when there's no evidence this is true) or it's apparent the therapist doesn't view you as part of the solution, that therapist won't be effective at helping your child. You need a therapist who will create a collaborative relationship with you. To achieve this goal, a therapist should assume you're ready, willing, and able to help your child.

Therapy and Adoption

Be sure to find out the following about a therapist you're considering:

- Is he or she an adoptive parent, adopted person, or birth parent? The only way to know is to ask the therapist. It doesn't automatically disqualify a person if she fits one of these categories, but you should be aware of it, and realize there may be conscious or unconscious biases at work.

- How does the therapist feel about adoption? If she believes all adopted children are emotionally disturbed, find another therapist. If she feels love conquers all problems and adoption always works out wonderfully, get another therapist. To get an idea of what a therapist thinks, make a nonjudgmental statement such as, "Some adopted children have problems." If the therapist says most adopted children have problems, that's a bias. If she says none have problems, that's also a bias. Get another therapist.

- Is the therapist knowledgeable about adoption? Few are, so don't make this a precondition for a therapist. (And don't assume if a therapist is an adoptive parent, adopted person, or birth parent, that she knows much about adoption. She may know little other than her own experience.) In fact, as therapist Ken Watson wrote in a 2002 issue of *Adoptalk*, a therapist not educated about adoption may be better. Said Watson, "If you put in some time educating your therapist, [then] a good therapist who's interested in adoption may ultimately be more effective than a less competent therapist who's sensitive to adoption."

Some Dos and Don'ts About Therapy

Here are some basic dos and don'ts about therapy after you've decided therapy is needed and you've found a therapist for your child.

- Don't expect immediate results. Emotional problems often take time to build up, and it's rare you'll find a "quick fix" for them. On the other hand, after a few sessions, ask the therapist for a guesstimate on about how many therapy sessions your child may need before improvement may be expected.

- Expect to participate in some part of your child's therapy. Some parents think if they drop the child off for therapy on a regular basis, the child and the therapist will work out all the problems between the two of them. Instead, therapists for older children need involved parents. If your child is school-age or younger, parents are often even more actively involved in therapy.

- Don't expect the therapist to tell you everything your child says and does in private sessions. Even children are entitled to some confidentiality. Do expect, however, that the therapist will tell you if your child needs something from you and whether your child is progressing, worsening, or staying the same.

- After a few sessions, if the child has an emotional problem, the therapist will explain what she thinks it is. If you're given a medical diagnosis, don't fixate on the diagnosis and search for hours on the Internet for information. The Internet can be a wonderful resource, but it's also replete with wrong information. (Read more about this topic in the Appendix.) The therapist may, however, be able to suggest several books that could help you understand the problem.

- Expect highs and lows as your child continues in therapy. Because attention is being paid to her problem, your child may improve at first, and then relapse. This doesn't mean the therapist has failed. Therapy isn't a linear path from emotional illness to full health. Sometimes there are problems on the way. The key is whether you see significant improvements over time.

- Some therapists may recommend medications, usually starting at a low dose. Some religious groups actively oppose medication, but research has shown that many times medication can help a child greatly, particularly with problems such as depression, ADHD (attention deficit hyperactivity disorder), OCD, and so forth. In contrast, if parents are having a relationship problem with a child unrelated to depression or another emotional problem, medications are generally not indicated.

Coping with Your Own Negative Feelings

It's normal to have feelings of anger, anxiety, and other emotions related to a child's emotional problems. Many parents wonder if they shouldn't have adopted at all or not adopted this child. It doesn't mean you're a bad parent if you have these feelings. What matters is what you do to help your child cope with her problems. One way to help is to not bury your feelings but deal with them. Sometimes you need therapy yourself to deal with these strong feelings.

Feelings of Failure

Keep in mind that you can't be a perfect parent, and you've tried to do a good job in raising your child and will continue to try hard. It's easy to fall into the trap of thinking your child's problems must be all your fault. Adoptive parents may worry about what they should have done or not done. Parents whose children weren't adopted and have emotional problems also worry. Don't obsess on fault-finding. Instead, focus on solution-seeking.

Feelings of Helplessness

Many parents feel very out of control when their children suffer from emotional problems. Maybe you're excellent at your job or at home, and now you have this problem that is beyond your resolution and that requires others to help you. This is not an easy thing to accept. Therapy may help you resolve these feelings.

Feelings of Depression and Anxiety

If you feel very sad, day after day, or start to have suicidal thoughts that can't be driven away, see your physician and/or a therapist. It's very common for parents with emotionally ill children to need therapy to help them cope. It doesn't mean you're weak or crazy or that you made your child weak or crazy. It means you're struggling with a difficult problem. It's also true that antidepressants might help you.

Wondering If You're the Wrong Parent for This Child

You may wonder if your child would have been better off with different adoptive parents. You may speculate that maybe the child shouldn't have been adopted because he'd have been happier with his biological parents. Actively challenge these negative statements to yourself. You also need to accept that you must deal with the situation as it is, not how things might have been if other choices had been made in the past. In most cases, if someone else had adopted your child, that person would be struggling too.

Dealing with Your Life Partner's Reactions

If you and your child live with your spouse or with someone you regard as a life partner, then you're both affected by a child's emotional problems.

How You Think He or She *Should* Feel

Your spouse or partner may not feel as you do about the emotional problems your child has. You may feel your partner should be taking your child's emotional problem more seriously or differently. Sometimes your assessment of your partner's attitude can impede your progress in helping your child.

Two adults parenting the same child may react very differently to a child's problems. This doesn't mean one adult is right and the other is wrong. What's needed is an accommodation between adults, not a lockstep agreement. For example, maybe your partner is more optimistic than you are and thinks the problem will work itself out. He may see worrying as nonproductive. If you're convinced he's wrong, don't attack his beliefs, but point out facts that indicate that a real problem is present.

For example, if your son Jason stole some items from a friend, and a few days later set fire to his bedspread, and you can think of more examples of serious problem behaviors, point them all out to your partner. Tell a partner who's said everything's just fine that these are *not* normal behaviors. Let's say these problem behaviors seem to be escalating. Several months ago, Jason wasn't behaving like this. Now he's acting out almost every day.

Point this fact out too. Of course, before you take your child to a therapist, be sure to take him to your pediatrician first, who can help you determine if therapy is warranted.

Although an emotionally ill child needs a therapist, this doesn't necessarily mean your partner will be enthusiastic. For many people, it's hard to discuss family problems with a stranger. It can be difficult to accept advice from a stranger about personal problems, even when she has an M.D. or a Ph.D. However, as long as your partner is willing for the child to see a therapist, and willing to participate in at least some therapy sessions, don't complain that his enthusiasm isn't as intense as yours.

The Parental Status of Your Partner

If your partner adopted the child with you, you both need to share in the decision making on how to help the child. If he or she is a person you live with but isn't an adoptive parent, you'll need to work with your partner, but must ultimately make the tough decisions yourself. This doesn't mean partners who are nonspouses aren't important. They are usually very important in helping you by listening to you, advising you, and bolstering you in the tough times. They are also important to your child.

Appendix

Helpful Resources

IF YOU'D LIKE to learn more about adoption, many resources can help. There's good material to read, and there are also adoptive parent groups and other organizations with useful information. In addition, there's a wealth of information on the Internet, although be sure to retain a healthy skepticism about what you read there. This appendix describes adoption resources and offers suggestions on using the Internet effectively.

Adoptive Parent Groups

Often people think of adoptive parent groups as organizations effective at helping them adopt a child, but they abandon the group after they've successfully adopted, seeing no further reason to attend any meetings. However, adoptive parent groups can provide excellent opportunities to learn more about adoption as well as meet parents with children about the same age as yours. This can be very helpful for your children.

Although there are many adopted children in the United States and Canada, most children don't make a big deal out of their adoptedness, so other children don't know who among them is adopted. Yet at the same time, many children would *like* to meet other adopted kids. One way to arrange such a meeting is through parent group picnics and parties.

Several years ago, my coauthor led an adoptive parent group. At a holiday party, she overheard one child say to another, "So you're adopted too!

I think almost every kid in this room was adopted!" The child's mother later told my coauthor that the child, an eight-year-old who had been adopted in the past year from foster care, had been somewhat negative about being adopted before she went to the party. Afterwards, she had a different outlook. She realized she wasn't the only adopted person in the world and the other adopted kids were just regular kids. That helped considerably.

You can locate an adoptive parent group in your area in several ways. Local social workers at adoption agencies in your area may be able to help. In addition, the National Adoption Information Clearinghouse publishes a National Adoption Directory with state-by-state listings of adoption agencies, parent groups, and other organizations. The Directory is also a free searchable database online. (However, it costs $25 if you order it by mail.) Contact the NAIC at

NAIC
330 C Street SW
Washington, DC 20447
Phone: 888-251-0075 (toll-free)
Website: calib.com/naic

Some adoptive parent groups are very large, while others have only a handful of members. In addition, some groups concentrate on children adopted from China, Russia, or other countries, while others concentrate on single adoptive parents who've adopted their children from anywhere.

Stars of David International, Inc., is a group for Jewish and part-Jewish adoptive families. Contact them at

Stars of David International, Inc.
3175 Commercial Avenue, Suite 100
Northbrook, IL 60062
Phone: 847-509-9929
Website: starsofdavid.org

The Adoptive Parents Committee is a large group in New York with many chapters. Contact them at

Adoptive Parents Committee
P.O. Box 3535
Church Street Station
New York, NY 10008
Phone: 917-432-0234
Website: adoptiveparents.org

Reading About Adoption and Parenting

If you'd like to continue your reading about adoptive parenting, you're in luck because good material is available.

Books

There are a variety of books about adoptive parenting in particular and parenting in general, including too many to list them all in this appendix. There are also numerous children's books about adoption. One popular children's book, for children up to about second grade, is *Tell Me Again About the Night I Was Born*, by Jamie Lee Curtis, which is among the books listed here.

Adoptive Parenting Books

- *Adoption Across Borders: Serving the Children in Transracial and Intercountry Adoptions* by Rita J. Simon and Howard Altstein (Rowman and Littlefield Publishers, 2000).

  A book that very comprehensively covers studies of children adopted in transracial and international adoptions. Clearly explains key research.

- *Inside Transracial Adoption* by Gail Steinberg and Beth Hall (Perspectives Press, 2000).

  A helpful book for parents who have adopted children in transracial and international adoptions, offering practical advice.

- *Parenting the Hurt Child: Helping Adoptive Families Heal and Grow* by Gregory C. Keck, Ph.D., and Regina M. Kupecky, L.S.W. (Piñon Press, 2002).

  This book offers practical and helpful advice for parents whose children were abused before they were adopted.

- *Talking to Young Children About Adoption* by Mary Watkins and Susan Fisher (Yale University Press, 1993).

  This book concentrates on preschool children, offering many situations and how parents handle them in different ways, as well as offering a psychological perspective.

- *Tell Me Again About the Night I Was Born* by Jamie Lee Curtis (HarperCollins Juvenile Books, 1996).

  A charming children's story about adoption.

Parenting Books

- *1-2-3 Magic: Effective Discipline for Children 2–12* by Thomas W. Phelan, Ph.D. (Child Management, 1996).

  A useful and practical book for parents about behavior management.

- *Potty Training for Dummies* by Diane Stafford and Jennifer Shoquist, M.D. (New York: Wiley Publishing, 2002).

  Everything you need to know about toilet training.

- *SOS! Help for Parents Book* by Lynn Clark, Ph.D. (Parents Press, 1996).

  A helpful parental guide.

Adoptive Families Magazine

The premier adoption magazine is *Adoptive Families* magazine. It's based in New York and subscribed to by thousands of adoptive parents and others interested in adoption. *Adoptive Families* offers a balance of articles for people who have adopted their children from the United States and from other countries, and includes information on a myriad of different parenting topics.

The magazine also provides up-to-date information on state and federal laws affecting adoption, as well as newsworthy articles about adoption. *Adoptive Families* also publishes an extremely valuable annual *Adoption Guide*, oriented to those seeking to adopt for the first time or again. For more information, contact

Adoptive Families
42 West 38th Street, Suite 901
New York, NY 10018
Phone: 800-372-3300 (toll-free)
Website: adoptivefamilies.com

Another useful source of information for adoptive parents who have adopted children in the United States and other countries is *Adoption Today* magazine. For more information, contact

Adoption Today
541 East Garden Drive, Unit N
Windsor, CO 80550
Phone: 888-924-6736
Website: adoptinfo.net

The Internet

The Internet is both a wonderful and a terrible place for parents seeking information about adoption. It's wonderful because there's a wealth of information at your fingertips in the privacy of your own home. The Internet is also a vehicle enabling you to connect with other parents who may be wondering about the same issues as you—or maybe they've resolved them in a creative way that would work for you too! Some websites are general parenting sites that may or may not include information on adoption, while others concentrate specifically on adoptive parenting. You can also purchase books about adoption online at such sites as barnesandnoble .com, Amazon.com, and at many other online booksellers.

The Internet is also a terrible place for adoptive parents, because it's crowded with more information than you could possibly wade through, much of it contradictory. (Even smart researchers disagree with each other on many adoption issues.) Sometimes the information is wrong, as when people report mistaken or old information.

Finding Congenial Sites

Most people enjoy reading information placed on websites that they've read about or found on a "search engine" such as google.com. The worst way to find adoption websites that may interest you is to do a search using the word "adoption." You'll be so overwhelmed by so many sites that you might just give up before you even start. Even "adopted children" will give you too many potential sites to check out.

Whatever search engine you use, such as google.com, yahoo.com, or others, try to limit the number of "hits" you'll get in a search by using targeted words. For example, if you're interested in more information on explaining adoption to your child, use such a phrase as "explaining adoption" (within quotation marks, as shown). After you experiment with different words and phrases, you'll learn how to find the information that you seek.

The listserv is another option for many people. A listserv is a (usually free) special interest group of members that generally offers you the option of receiving all messages sent by all members by e-mail or receiving a weekly narrative of all the messages. Yahoo offers many different listservs. When an e-mail is sent by one person, it can be read by anyone in the group, unless it is not sent through the listserv.

Yahoo groups have many different adoption listservs to choose from, including a large group for parents who are adopting or have already adopted from China (with over ten thousand members as of this writing!), as well as smaller groups for single parents who've adopted from Guatemala. Altogether, I located 302 different possible listservs about adoption on Yahoo in 2003. To join Yahoo, you must provide basic information about yourself, such as your name, address, and so forth. For further information, go to http://groups.yahoo.com.

The Importance of Being Careful

I think it's necessary in any discussion of the Internet to mention the problem of confidentiality. Many adoptive parents are eager to share their stories and problems with others; however, if the information is shared in a readable domain open to the public, it may be there for a long time, even years. As a rule of thumb, don't leave any information about yourself or your family if you would mind seeing it published on page one of the *New York Times* or your local newspaper.

Adoption Organizations Online

Here's a brief listing of the websites of some adoption organizations not previously mentioned:

Adoption.com
adoption.com

American Academy of Adoption Attorneys
adoptionattorneys.org

American Academy of Pediatrics adoption section
aap.org/sections/adoption

Comeunity Adoption Support
comeunity.com

Dave Thomas Foundation for Adoption
davethomasfoundationforadoption.org

Evan B. Donaldson Adoption Institute
adoptioninstitute.org

Families for Russian and Ukrainian Adoption
frua.org

Families with Children from China
fwcc.org

International Concerns Committee for Children
iccadopt.org

Joint Council on International Children's Services
jcics.org

Latin American Parents Association
lapa.com

National Adoption Center
adopt.org

National Council for Adoption
adoptioncouncil.org

National Resource Center for Special Needs Adoption
spaulding.org

North American Council on Adoptable Children (NACAC)
nacac.org

BIBLIOGRAPHY

Adamec, Christine. *The Adoption Option Complete Handbook 2000–2001* (Rocklin, CA: Prima Publishing, 1999).

——. *Is Adoption for You? The Information You Need to Make the Right Choice* (New York: John Wiley and Sons, 1998).

Adamec, Christine, and William L. Pierce, Ph.D. *The Encyclopedia of Adoption* (New York: Facts On File, Inc., 2000).

Adesman, Andrew. "Russian Adoption: Assessing the Risk—'Red Flags' vs. 'Red Herrings,'" *Chosen Child* 2, no. 3 (January 2000):35–39.

Benson, Peter L., Ph.D., Anu R. Sharma, Ph.D., and Eugene C. Roehlkepartain. *Growing Up Adopted: A Portrait of Adolescents and Their Families* (Minneapolis, MN: The Search Institute, 1994).

Bohman, Michael. *Adopted Children and Their Families* (Stockholm, Sweden: Proprius, 1970).

Bothun, Linda. *When Friends Ask About Adoption* (Chevy Chase, MD: Swan Publications, 1996).

Bowlby, John. *Attachment and Loss: Volume III: Loss* (New York: Basic Books, 1980).

——. *Maternal Care and Mental Health* (Geneva, Switzerland: World Health Organization, 1951).

Derdeyn, Andre P., M.D., and Charles L. Graves, M.D. "Clinical Vicissi-tudes of Adoption," *Child and Adolescent Psychiatric Clinics of North America* 7, no. 2 (April 1998):373–378.

Duyme, Michel, Annick-Camille Cumaret, and Stanislaw Tomkiewicz. "How Can We Boost IQs of 'Dull Children'?: A Late Adoption Study," *Proceedings of the National Academy of Sciences USA* 96 (July 1999): 8790–8794.

Eyer, Diane E. *Mother-Infant Bonding: A Scientific Fiction* (New Haven, CT: Yale University Press, 1992).

Freivalds, Susan. "Nature and Nurture: A New Look at How Families Work," *Adoptive Families* 35, no. 2 (March/April 2002):28–30.

Gray, Deborah D. *Attaching in Adoption: Practical Tools for Today's Parents* (Indianapolis, IN: Perspectives Press, Inc., 2002).

Grotevant, Harold D., Ph.D., principal investigator. "Adoptive Families: Longitudinal Outcomes for Adolescents. Final Report to the William Grant Foundation," April 30, 2001.

Groza, Victor, and Karen F. Rosenberg, editors. *Clinical and Practice Issues in Adoption* (Westport, CT: Praeger, 1998).

Haugaard, Jeffrey H. "Is Adoption a Risk Factor for the Development of Risk Problems?" *Clinical Psychology Review* 18, no. 1 (1998):47–69.

Hjern, Anders, Frank Lindblad, and Bo Vinnerljung. "Suicide, Psychiatric Illness, and Social Maladjustment in Intercountry Adoptees in Sweden: A Cohort Study," *Lancet* 360 (August 10, 2002):443–448.

Howe, David. *Patterns of Adoption: Nature, Nurture and Psychosocial Development* (London, England: Blackwell Science, 1998).

Keck, Gregory C., Ph.D., and Regina M. Kupecky, L.S.W. *Parenting the Hurt Child: Helping Adoptive Families Heal and Grow* (Colorado Springs, CO: Piñon Press, 2002).

Klaus, M., et al. "Maternal Attachment: Importance of the First Postpartum Days," *New England Journal of Medicine* 286, no. 9 (March 1972):460–463.

McNamara, Joan, and Bernard H. McNamara. *Adoption and the Sexually Abused Child* (Portland, ME: Human Services Development Institute, University of Southern Maine, 1990).

Nickman, Steven L. *The Adoption Experience: Stories and Commentaries* (New York: Julian Messner, 1985).

Nickman, Steven L., M.D., and Robert Ewis, M.S.W. "Adoptive Families and Professionals: When Experts Make Things Worse," *Journal of the American Academy of Child and Adolescent Psychiatry* 33, no. 5 (June 1994):753–755.

Quarles, Christopher S., and Jeffrey H. Brodie. "Primary Care of International Adoptees," *American Family Physician*, December 1998. Available online at aafp.org./afp/981200ap/quarles.html.

Raynor, Lois. *The Adopted Child Comes of Age* (London, England: George Allen and Unwin, 1980).

Rutter, Michael, and the English and Romanian Adoptees (ERA) Study Team. "Developmental Catch-Up, and Deficit, Following Adoption After Severe Global Early Privation," *Journal of Child Psychology and Psychiatry and Allied Disciplines* 39, no. 4 (1998):465–476.

Schecter, Marshall D., M.D., et al. "Observations on Adopted Children," *Archives of General Psychiatry* 3 (July 1960):21–32.

Simmel, Cassandra, et al. "Externalizing Symptomatology Among Adoptive Youth: Prevalence and Preadoption Risk Factors," *Journal of Abnormal Child Psychology* 29, no. 1 (2001):37–60.

Simon, Rita J., and Howard Altstein. *Adoption Across Borders: Serving the Children in Transracial and Intercountry Adoptions* (Lanham, MD: Rowman and Littlefield Publishers, Inc., 2000).

Smith, Dorothy W., and Laurie Nehls Sherwen. *Mothers and Their Adopted Children: The Bonding Process* (New York: Tiresias Press, 1983).

Smith, Peter K., Helen Cowie, and Mark Blades. *Understanding Children's Development* (Oxford, England: Blackwell, 2003).

Stafford, Diane, and Jennifer Shoquist, M.D. *Potty Training for Dummies* (New York: Wiley Publishing, 2002).

Steinberg, Gail, and Beth Hall. *Inside Transracial Adoption* (Indianapolis, IN: Perspectives Press, 2000).

U.S. Census Bureau. "Adopted Children and Stepchildren: 2000," U.S. Department of Commerce, Economics and Statistics Administration, U.S. Census Bureau, August 2003.

Virdis, Raffaele, et al. "Precocious Puberty in Girls Adopted from Developing Countries," *Archives of Disease in Childhood* 78 (1998):152–154.

Watson, Ken. "A Few Thoughts on Choosing an Effective Adoption Therapist," *Adoptalk*, Summer 2002:6.

Zeanah, Charles H., Anna T. Smyke, and Alina Dumitrescu. "Attachment Disturbances in Young Children: II: Indiscriminate Behavior and Institutional Care," *Journal of the American Academy of Child and Adolescent Psychiatry* 41, no. 8 (August 1, 2002): 983–989.

INDEX

Behavior(s)
  annoying but typical, 98
  consequences of, 97
  coping with common, 93, 128–29
  distinguishing between normal and
     abnormal, 97–98, 203–6
  fear of losing parents' love over
     obnoxious, 123
  frequency of, 98
  harmful, 98
  paranoid, 205
  praising good, 92–93
  problems with, in adopted children,
     11–12, 17–18, 61–66
Believability of myth, 25
Biological child, having, either before or
    after adopting, 127
Biracial issues, 187, 195–96
Birth history, 163
Birth mothers
  adoption as choice of, 20
  age of, at time of adoption, 19–20
  change of mind by, 156
  concerns of child on return of, 139–40
  in foreign adoptions, 20
  meeting, 104
  reasons for choosing adoption, 102–3,
     148–50
Birth order, 126
  changing, 131
Birth parents
  adopted adult search for, 20–21
  alcohol or drug use in, 201
  attempts to reclaim children, 18–19
  avoiding negativity about, 143–44
  choice of adoption by, 18
  contact with, and open adoptions, 36
  decision to see, 140–41
  depiction of, as saints, 143
  fear of turning into, 121–22
  fears about meeting, 123
  foster care and, 21–22
  inabilities of, to parent child, 103
  locating, 36
  similarity to adopted children, 12–13
Blindness, 183

Bohman, Michael, 16
Bonding, 69–84
  by adopted children, 34–36
  background of, 71–72
  defined, 70
  by foreign adopted children, 22
  strengthening, 83–84
Books, 217–18
Boundaries, 73
  violations of, 59–60
Bowlby, John, 71, 76, 77
Breaks, taking regular, 89
Breastfeeding, 85, 90
Brodie, Jeffrey H., 178
Bulimia, 64
Bully, 205

Children. *See also* Adopted children
  coping with common behaviors of
    small, 93
  former attachments of, 78
  nonadopted, 147
  potential needs of new, 131
  thinking about adopting another,
    130–32
  unattached, 81
Children and Adults with Attention
    Deficit Disorder (CHADD), 208–9
Child with special needs, gratefulness
    and, 15
Chosen child mistake, 149–50
Closed adoption, 13–14, 127
Cognitive-behavioral therapy (CBT), 89
Colic, 5
Common sense
  defined, 3–4
  importance of, 5
  perceptions versus, 4
  retaining, about attachment, 73
  risks of parenting without, xiii–xiv
Common sense parenting, xii–xiv
  key elements of, 9–10
Communication
  with adolescents, 153–54
  with child, 142–45, 167–70
  with friends, 160